Liner Shipping in 2025

By Lars Jensen

Liner Shipping in 2025

How to survive and thrive

Vespucci Maritime Publishing

Lars Jensen

Liner Shipping in 2025

How to survive and thrive

ISBN: 978-1543045161

1st edition, 2017

Table of Contents

Preface

In the past 20 years many industries have been subjected to business disruption. Although the term "disruption" is usually vaguely defined, it is easily recognized when seen in retrospect. Digital photography disrupted the traditional film photography, online streaming disrupted the video rental business and Amazon disrupted the bookseller industry and then proceeded on to larger pastures. Of course these are just a couple of the most simple and well-known examples, with a plethora of other examples available from the past 20 years.

Furthermore, business disruption is not a new phenomenon. The automobile disrupted the horse trading industry. European maritime developments and the voyages of discovery by European seafarers disrupted the overland Silkroad traders. The British textile mills coming out of the industrialization disrupted the textile producing industry in the Bay of Bengal.

In essence, whoever claims disruption to be a new phenomenon associated with the current transformation of global business markets lacks historic perspective. But the fact that disruption has always been around does not diminish its relevance. But it does provide guidance into what we should expect. And therein lies the key to understand the choices we are faced with.

Disruption does not automatically mean that all existing industry players will disappear. Nor does it imply that all players need to change into identical companies with identical business models. Quite the contrary, the disruption we are witnessing the early phases of will leave ample opportunity for differentiation – but it will be of a different kind than we are used to.

Disruption means that significant parts of the way the industry operates will change. This in turn will force industry stakeholders to either change themselves or be forced out of the market. It implies that a plethora of new opportunities will present themselves, creating new markets for both existing industry players as well as newcomers.

But equally it implies that choices have to be made. Choices which will determine the trajectory upon which the industry players will launch themselves over the coming years. Not doing anything is in itself also a choice. Similarly a hesitation to act, is a choice. In some cases the uncertainties may be so large, that hesitation appears to be the best strategy – but it may also prove to be the opposite.

What, then, is the purpose of this book? There is no shortage of books looking at disruption as a general phenomenon, with the term possibly being one of the most hyped business-terms in recent years. Therefore this book is not a general introduction to, or overview of, disruption. Neither is it an academic treatise heavy in tables, graphs and figures with myriads of references.

This book aims at providing fundamental understanding and inspiration for anyone wanting to partake in the disruption of the maritime liner shipping industry over the next 10 years. This includes shipping lines, cargo owners, freight forwarders, ports, terminals, government authorities, service providers and the whole ecosystem of companies which makes up a modern supply chain.

It is aimed equally at the newcomers to liner shipping who may not fully understand the idiosyncrasies of the industry, and therefore which barriers exist to be broken, as well as aimed at the experienced industry insiders who are well aware of the intricacies of the industry but who want to lift themselves above the day-to-day challenges and get a glimpse of the landscape lying ahead.

The book is aimed to serve as a guide with which to frame the context and questions every company involved in liner shipping need to ask themselves, as well as provide guidance on which directions are long-term viable, and which ones are ultimately lost causes.

Many different parts of the industry will be changing at the same time, and it is not possible to "rank" these elements in a linear fashion. Rather multiple elements will interact with other, and each section of the book will be dealing with different elements. The sequence of these in the book does not signal a hierarchy, nor does it signal a sequence through which the changes will happen. Instead each individual company needs to ascertain their own position in relation to each element, and based on this determine their own sequence of changes.

Obviously, such an aim raises a range of fundamental questions such as: Will the industry by disrupted at all, how will it be disrupted and by whom will it be disrupted?

Predicting future events is by no means an accurate science, and the forecasts of the developments in store for the liner shipping industry provided herein is based on my own strategic analysis of past and current developments. This is background knowledge and analysis which have been developed over the past 16 years, having been at the forefront of analysing the liner shipping industry.

My fundamental view is that the industry is indeed facing a profound change over the next 10-20 years. It is not a matter of whether the industry as such will survive – it will persist, although growth rates and geographical trade dispersal might indeed be questioned. However, the crucial question any company involved in liner shipping today have to ask themselves, is whether they themselves will survive as a company – or rather, what it will take to transform and adapt to a new reality.

Make no mistake – the industry will indeed both survive and thrive, but no individual company is likely to thrive, let alone survive, if they do not change materially.

Lars Jensen

Copenhagen

February 2017

Will Liner Shipping be disrupted?

Whether the liner shipping industry is even about to be disrupted is a critical question that must be addressed at the outset. And before we explore that question, it is necessary to define what "Liner Shipping" is taken to mean in the context of this book.

Liner Shipping in this context is defined as the shipment of containerized cargo on vessels predominantly operating on fixed schedules, as well as the necessary operations in place to facilitate the transportation. This means that, for example, passenger and RoRo ferries, which technically speaking also operate on fixed routes with fixed schedules and as such constitute liner trade, are not the primary focal points for this outlook to 2025.

However, some associated industries which are necessary to facilitate the movement of containerized cargo are included in the scope. The most important industries are the ports and terminals, the inland transportation to/from the ports, whether by truck, rail or barge as well as the freight forwarders and NVOCC in so much as they move full container loads.

If the claim is to be made that Liner Shipping is about to become disrupted, we need to know the current baseline of the industry in order to know what exactly it is we are about to change away from. This baseline is laid out in more detail in later chapters, but the core of the matter is that several external parameters beyond the control of the liner shipping industry are changing.

Macro-economic and demographic shifts are changing the trade patterns, causing the shipping lines to change as well. To put it perhaps too simplistically, the shipping lines are free to choose where to place their transshipment hubs – but the origin and destination of the actual cargo is beyond their control, and the general pattern of origins and destinations are changing.

On the surface it also appears as if IT developments will be changing the industry, but in reality it is more fundamental than IT. Industries which get disrupted are not disrupted because of a technological gadget or a now application. They are disrupted because that new gadget or application fundamentally changes the processes related to the production, distribution, sale and use of the product. In liner shipping we have a large range of intermediary steps, and for companies outside the industry, this appears to be begging for disruption.

In a relative simple example, the shipment of a container from an inland point in one continent to an inland point in another continent could involve one major shipping line, two local feeder lines, four container ports, one rail company, one barge company, two trucking companies, two local freight forwarders, two customs authorities, two container depots and three banks. All of these have different processes and different systems.

Once more – this is literally begging for a company to disrupt the industry and do away with the complexity. However, large parts of that complexity is not easy to remove overnight once the details underneath are contemplated, and hence any disruption is bound to take time. Quite a number of companies have appeared during 2015-2016 with visions of disrupting the industry. However, it is also clear that they have all chosen different partial elements of the full chain, and they want to disrupt these individual elements, not the entire chain. That in itself is a clear indication of the daunting task of transforming the entire industry.

For the shipping lines this means that they have the opportunity to drive the transformation themselves. When we are looking towards 2025, transformation is a more apt description than disruption. Whilst we will likely see a number of the new companies which focus on disrupting individual elements succeed, the change of the entire industry will be a more protracted affair. However, the direction is clear

– increasingly each of the complexities will become streamlined and governed by more simple processes, and the end point is an industry in 2025 which will have been transformed significantly compared to the way it operates today.

Tactical versus Strategic Challenges

2016 was clearly a very poor year for the liner shipping companies with billion dollar losses all around. And losses are not the exception, rather they appear to be the norm in an industry which has mainly been destroying value for the owners over the past 10 years.

Clearly this pressure brings with it a set of urgent challenges to be met – and the collapse of Korean owned Hanjin in August 2016 demonstrated clearly what happens when these challenges are not handled successfully.

However, when companies are contemplating changes toward 2025 and beyond it is necessary to distinguish between tactical and strategic challenges.

This book is primarily concerned with developments which will unfold over a 10-year horizon, and therefore the strategic challenges associated with this transformation. That, however, should not be taken as an indication that the tactical challenges should be ignored on the grounds that the "big picture" is more important. It does, however, mean that when liner shipping companies choose solutions to their tactical problems, they should do so with an eye towards whether these solutions, in addition to solving the immediate problem, also supports the long-term solution of the strategic challenges.

It is important to stress this differentiation, as presently the industry does indeed face a number of pressing tactical problems which, if left unresolved, will lead to the demise of many companies.

As the whole purpose of the book is to outline the strategic challenges, and propose relevant solutions to them, this small chapter is meant to focus on the differentiation so often used in business literature: What is important? And what is urgent?

The matter of what is important is what will be outlined through this book. And in this context "important" is seen through the lens of achieving business success over the next decade.

However, problems clearly abound which are urgent, and if left unchecked will bring a company to be eliminated long before they can realize the benefits of a 10-year transformation. It is therefore important to note that all the long-term challenges which must be addressed does not take precedence over the resolution of the urgent, tactical, problems.

But, conversely, any liner shipping company which aspires to be a part of the industry in 2025 also need to carefully assess how they resolve the tactical problems. The tools employed can take many forms, and the prism within which they should be evaluated is the degree to which they not only solve the tactical problems, but also whether they, at best, support the long-term transformation or, as a minimum, do not prevent such a transformation.

This might all appear somewhat abstract, hence it can be beneficial to look at a couple of practical examples to illustrate the point.

The extremely low freight rates have led to unprecedented losses for a range of container lines. Clearly they need to take steps to curb the losses and revert to profitability. This is an issue which cannot await a long-term solution in the 5-10 year time span, a point which was brought home to all market players by the collapse of Hanjin.

However, whilst the need to revert to profitability clearly is a tactical issue, shipping lines need to contemplate whether the tools they employ will support or hinder the needed long-term changes. Several tools can be chosen to assist in the process, and the point here is not to list exhaustive tactical solutions but rather to point out the impact of tactical solutions.

One approach involves the reduction of costs, but this is too much of an abstraction. The question is how such a cost reduction is to be achieved.

One approach could be to outsource key functions to service centers in lower-cost countries, incidentally an avenue many shipping lines have pursued for a number of years. However, we are at a point where the question must be asked: If you can define a task with such clarity that it can be shifted to a low-cost standardized environment, then why not automate it instead?

The up-front costs of automation might prove prohibitive given the current tactical problems, and hence the outsourcing would be a more viable short-term solution. However, even in that case we are at a point in time where any kind of standardization or outsourcing should be seen as only a stepping stone and not as the final solution. This will be covered in more detail in the sections pertaining to process management as well as automation. The point here being that the short-term action of outsourcing might be the right one, but should be done with a longer-term plan in mind.

Another example would be an approach whereby the shipping line would seek to raise freight rates based on the premise that they could negotiate better rates with the customers than their competitors, especially with smaller customers who might not be as aware of the market conditions as the larger cargo owners.

Whilst this approach might indeed be met with short-term success, the shipping line in this case needs to be careful about how they do this. Significant parts of the container shipping markets are rapidly becoming transparent in terms of price formation, and hence an approach based on getting customers to agree on higher price due to better negotiation skills is likely to be met with only short-term success, but at the cost of deteriorating customer relationships.

These are of course very simplistic examples, and as mentioned are by no means intended to be exhaustive. They are instead intended to provide a mental framework for the coming parts of this book. It is a mental framework wherein the tactical challenges facing the liner shipping industry are not forgotten or ignored, but are placed temporarily on hold. Once we have a clear overview of the strategic challenges, and the ways in which to address them, then the tactical challenges can be re-assessed from the point of view that it is insufficient "only" to resolve these problems. It is equally necessary that the chosen tactical solutions should be stepping stones towards meeting the strategic challenges as well.

The current market status

In order to understand the current status of the liner shipping markets – and how they will evolve in the coming decade – it is necessary to understand how the market got to its current state. To do this, one must look at three different timescales. The first time scale stretches over 60 years since the inception of the container itself. The second time scale stretches over the period roughly from the mid-1990s to the financial crisis in 2008. The third time scale stretches from the financial crisis until the present day – and actually a couple of years further on.

The longest timescale stretching from the shipment of the first container in 1956 to the present date is important because it goes to the very heart of the lifetime development of any industry. At first an industry starts out very small until traction is gained. This was the case from 1956 until the late 1960s. During this period there were no standards, not even in terms of the size of container used, and hence growth was limited. By the end of the 1960s the current 20/40' standards were solidified, setting the scale for a rapid expansion.

This brought the industry to the second phase of any successful industry lifecycle: Growth. Initially the growth was driven by the very containerization process itself as breakbulk cargo was moved into steel boxes. During the 1990's this was gradually overtaken by a second driver, outsourcing of production. This brings us to the second period of importance in the industry. As global outsourcing was gathering pace, it was not only the amounts of cargo which grew, but the distances over which they were transported also rose rapidly. Cargo which had already been outsourced from the USA to Mexico was now shifted to China. Equally, manufacturing which had relocated from North Europe to, for example, the Iberian Peninsula was now moved out to Asia. This growth necessitated a rapid escalation of the fleet of container vessels.

Further adding to this effect was the increasing trade imbalances. It is a fact that most trade lanes in the world are imbalanced. As an example, whenever two containers are shipped from Asia to the US, only one container with cargo is available for the return journey. The direction in which the majority of cargo is shipped is termed the head haul trade.

This means that the expansion of capacity must match demand growth in the head haul trade. During this period the trade imbalances grew, and hence capacity had to keep pace with the faster growing head haul demand and not with the overall global average demand growth.

In the 25 years from 1980 to 2005 global container shipping capacity grew 3 percentage points faster than global demand. Every year. Compounded over 25 years this means that in total, the nominal fleet capacity grew 110% more than the underlying number of containers which needed to be transported.

In itself this was not a problem, as the ever longer distances in combination with the increasing trade imbalances resulted in adequate vessel utilization on the key head haul trades. Of course the 25 years were not characterized by stability. The shipping markets have always been cyclical, and the container shipping industry is no different. But as an average view over the full 25 years, there was a reasonable balance between the rapid injection of new capacity, and the associated growth in demand on the head haul trades.

For the container shipping lines, it implied that they needed to have a strategy which could keep pace with this rapid growth. In terms of demand, the market exhibited an average growth of 8% annually during the 25 years, whereas capacity grew 11% annually. This is by any standards an exceptionally high growth rate to sustain for 25 years. The net effect was a fleet where the nominal capacity grew 13-fold from 1980 to 2005.

In such a rapidly growing competitive environment, this favoured companies whose main strength was the ability to finance such rapid growth along with a management culture supporting the rapid build-up of global infrastructure across scores of countries. Additionally, it favoured companies who were willing to order vessels on the assumption of high growth, even though such capacity was not needed at the time of ordering.

On the commercial side, the rapid growth meant that the need to truly compete for market share with other shipping lines was less important. Not that such competition did not happen, surely it did, however on balance it was of lesser importance. At an 8% annual market growth it was a challenge even to keep pace with natural organic growth. As in any industry, is more efficient to increase sales from existing customers, when possible, than it is to acquire new customers. Secondly, due to the rapid pace of outsourcing a large range of cargo owners suddenly found themselves in need of containerized shipping services, and the shipping lines could therefore target an entirely novel customer base. Hence the sales processes which developed naturally became skewed towards ensuring that a shipping line would grow with their existing customer base, as well as focused on bringing in new cargo owners as they began to shift their production overseas. Clearly some competition was also going on in terms of capturing other shipping lines' customers, however in the light of the rapid market growth there was less of a need to pursue this avenue.

All of this is not to say any of the shipping lines did anything wrong – quite the opposite. Any shipping line who could not successfully pursue this high growth strategy simply would not become a large global shipping line.

But at the core of this strategy was the fact that the industry was in the second phase of the industry lifecycle, growth. Any high growth process will at some point in time hit a point where such growth can no longer be sustained. The containerization process had essentially ran its course, with only minor cargo volumes, notably some reefer cargo, not yet being fully containerized. The main driver had shifted to become the outsourcing of manufacturing. A logical hypothesis would be that the pace of outsourcing would follow a traditional S-curve whereby uptake would initially be slow, then accelerate, reach an inflection point and then eventually taper off to reach a steady-state. A study was undertaken by the author of this book in 2004 focused on the Transpacific market to ascertain whether the developments were following such an S-shaped curve, and if it did, where was the inflection point and when would growth be reduced to a slower steady-state.

The result of the study was that the market was already at the inflection point. Rapid growth could be expected for a few more years, however once we got beyond 2010 the growth rates would subside significantly as the boost from outsourcing would be tapering off.

This outlook was well in line with the traditional lifecycle phases for any industry whereby the 2nd phase of growth is eventually replaced by a 3rd phase of maturity. The 3rd phase has much lower growth than the 2nd phase, and this is where successful companies need to shift their strategy away from the pursuit of rapid growth and onto process efficiency.

However, the industry participants, and most notably the shipping lines, did not recognize the underlying shift from the 2nd to the 3rd phase.

In the final years of 2006-2008 leading up to the financial crisis, the easy availability of financing led the shipping lines to order even larger amounts of capacity than previously. Whereas the norm had been that the orderbooks for shipyards were typically filled 2 years into the future, the state of affairs was that the yards had orders filling the books 3 years into the future at the time where the financial crisis impacted the industry. The orders which had already been placed would see the fleet expand by more than 50%.

Seen in the light of the preceding 25 years, such an expansion was not necessarily excessive. From the perspective of each individual shipping line it was seen as necessary in order to maintain their market position, and fully in line with the mindset that had proven successful for decades.

The financial crisis resulted in complete collapse of the container shipping markets, with 2009 seeing global container volumes decline by more than 10%. This was new territory as the container shipping markets had never experienced negative growth rates before. Even during the recessions in the early 1980's, the container shipping markets had seen positive demand growth.

The sudden decline in demand was then compounded by the continued delivery of new vessels, and during 2009 the shipping lines saw no other way out than to idle vessels. At the height of this process 10-12% of the global fleet of container vessels was idled. This helped bring some balance back into the supply/demand equation, and the markets began to recover in late 2009 and early 2010.

As the global economy emerged from the financial crisis, container volumes also came back. And consequently the idled vessels were brought back into service.

The problem was that the underlying growth for the container markets had indeed shifted from the 2nd to the 3rd phase of the industry's development, but when growth rates were seen against the backdrop of 2009 it appeared as if the "normal" market development had returned.

That the markets were anything but normal could be seen in the behaviour during late 2009 and 2010. Charter rates for vessels remained subdued, creating opportunities for a range of new shipping lines to start services based on using the low-priced vessels. And it was not just newcomers who saw opportunities. In a bold, but ultimately ill-fated, move Chilean shipping line CSAV went from being the world's 20th largest container line to becoming the 9th largest within a span of just a few months. This was driven by the intake of large amounts of cheap capacity, and clearly with the assumption that it would be possible to get enough cargo to fill the vessels.

These developments were a clear signal that despite the resurgence of the market there was an underlying structural overcapacity problem. But overcapacity was not new to an industry which had been cyclical not only since the invention of the container, but in essence for centuries. Hence shipping lines had not only become accustomed to occasional overcapacity, but had – successfully – relied on strategies which resulted in cyclical overcapacity. The strong underlying market growth then ensured that the overcapacity would be absorbed by organic growth in a relatively short timeframe.

But as 2010 progressed it was becoming clear that it was difficult to fill the vessels, and towards the end of 2010 fuel prices increased dramatically, essentially doubling since the beginning of 2009. Herewith the baseline was set for a stage in the development which continues to impact markets today. The combination of escalating fuel costs and increasing overcapacity led the carriers to the rational analysis that by slowing down the vessels they could both reduce the fuel expenses and absorb part of the overcapacity at the same time.

In the context of liner shipping, a service needs to have a round-trip sailing time measured in multiples of 7 days, as this provides customers with a regular weekly service. Slowing the vessels down has the effect of needing more vessels to service the same trade. In the most extreme cases, services which connected Asia with North Europe were gradually shifted from round trips lasting 56 days, using 8 vessels, to taking 77 days and using 11 vessels. The capital costs clearly increased as more vessels were used, but this was more than offset by the savings in fuel costs due to the much slower speed.

The carriers had therefore found a tool, termed slow steaming, with which to continue to absorb the deliveries of new vessels ordered before the financial crisis, even though the underlying demand did not warrant the introduction of such large amounts of capacity.

Cargo owners were not satisfied with this development, as it had the effect of prolonging their supply chains, but as carriers sought to combat both oversupply and non-compensatory freight rates the cargo owners were given no choice.

The non-compensatory freight rates were an effect of a price war the carriers were engaged in during the latter parts of 2010 as well as 2011. On the surface it was a fight for market share combined with an attempt to get the market to consolidate. Some liner shipping executives even stated publicly that there was an effort to drive weaker lines out of the market. These efforts proved fruitless, only to be realised in 2016.

In this environment of growing overcapacity, masked by the increased slow steaming, the step was taken to introduce a new vessel class. In February 2011, the largest container line, Maersk Line, announced the ordering of a series of vessels with a capacity of 18.000 TEU. Despite marketing efforts to the contrary, this development was -seen in - isolation not unique. It represented an increase in nominal vessel size of 16% versus the vessels which were until then the largest, and 30% versus what was more typically the largest vessels across a range of main carriers. They would bring significant unit cost savings, but in a historical context such steps had been seen, and absorbed, before. The problem was the chain of events it resulted in.

In a situation where all main shipping lines were seeking to reduce unit costs dramatically, Maersk Line appeared to be on the cusp of securing a solid competitive scale advantage. It quickly led to a few main competitors ordering vessels of a similar size, and then events snowballed.

Even though all market participants in 2013-15 were acutely aware of the rapidly escalating overcapacity in the market, most embarked on a path where they too ordered the new mega vessels ranging in size between 18.000-20.500 TEU. Nobody would have had doubts as to whether the market in the short term would be able to absorb this influx of capacity – it couldn't. Why then did they do it?

Essentially, they found themselves trapped in a market dynamic beyond their own control. Abstain from ordering mega vessels, and you would become the carrier who did not have a unit cost advantage once the markets stabilized. Join the ordering spree and you would exacerbate the structural overcapacity, pushing recovery even further into the future. Almost all major carriers joined the ordering spree of mega vessels, choosing between what they saw as two unpalatable options.

Around 2014, slow steaming was reaching the end of how many vessels could be absorbed through this method and consequently vessel utilization began to decline. The next counter-move by the shipping lines was termed "blank sailings". It is quite simply the ad-hoc cancellation of individual sailings when the vessel is assessed to have too poor a utilization. It temporarily improves the market balance, but at the cost of further alienating the cargo owners who experiences disruptions to their supply chain.

The escalating overcapacity manifested itself in the markets as rapidly eroding freight rates during 2014-2016, and in 2015-2016 this was compounded by the unexpected rapid drop in fuel prices. Lower fuel prices were not helping the shipping lines. Essentially the savings were passed on to the cargo owners through lower freight rates. At the same time, it had the effect of eroding the competitive advantage of the larger vessels, as this was to a large degree determined by fuel efficiency.

In 2016 these developments culminated during the 1st quarter where spot rates from China to South America reached just 50 USD for a full container and to Europe where a few customers were presented with offers for literally zero freight rates.

This triggered the largest round of consolidation seen amongst the main players in the industry. Eight top-20 carriers were slated to disappear as independent entities. Seven through acquisitions or mergers and one, Hanjin, through an outright bankruptcy. On top of that, the existing alliance structure was announced to be changed in April 2017, combining all main shipping lines into only 3 alliances on the deep-sea east-west trades.

This essentially brings us up to speed on where the shipping lines are right now, as well as how they got into the problem of severe overcapacity, which will take a long time to resolve. There are a significant amounts of nuances to this development which are also important in order to understand the events that will unfold over the next decade, but these will be dealt with in the subsequent sections. However, this outline of the developments serves as a context within which to add the additional nuance.

Before moving on, we should also take a closer look at how the cargo owners, freight forwarders, ports and terminals fit into this context.

As for the cargo owners, these are essentially the customers. These are the ones who have cargo in need of transportation. On the positive side, the cargo owners have experienced rapidly declining freight prices over the last 30 years, and at the same time they have benefitted from an increase in the number of ports globally to which they can easily ship their containerized goods.

Furthermore, due to the structural overcapacity, the customers have essentially had most of the pricing power since the financial crisis. This has enabled them to benefit financially from the cost saving measures brought about by the shipping lines.

However, whilst they have the power in terms of pricing, they have almost no influence on the quality of the product – at least not when quality is equated with aspects such as transit times, service frequency, reliability and cancelled sailings.

The severe erosion of freight rates has resulted in a liner shipping industry which, on average, have been destroying value for the owners over the past 10 years. This means that shipping lines are more focused on saving costs than on improving service quality. Compounding the problem is that the shipping lines mainly find customers to be unwilling to pay a premium for improved services.

And in the cases where customers might indeed be willing to pay for a premium service, the escalation in vessel sizes prevent them from taking advantage of this. As an example, if a customer is willing to pay a high price for a faster transit time, the shipping line might well conclude that this customer only brings 1.000 containers to the vessel, whereas the remaining 13.000 containers destined for the same vessel are booked by customers who are not willing to pay for a faster service.

The consequence is a global customer base which on one hand enjoys ever lower shipping costs, but at the same time suffer from lower service quality which imparts them with increasing costs elsewhere in the supply chain.

For the ports and terminals, the rapid growth in container markets have led to a rapid escalation in the sizes of container terminals. The largest ports today handle an average of more than one TEU *per second*. The growth rates seen for the ports over the decades have been even higher than for shipping lines, as the increased prevalence of hub-and-spoke dynamics have served to boost the number of times an average container is handled throughout its journey.

Essentially the container terminals have been exposed to the same dynamics as the shipping lines – to be successful it was necessary to have access to sufficient capital to keep pace with the rapid growth in volumes, as well as have the management structures in place to allow such growth to take place. The successful terminal operators are therefore ones which have been accustomed to be on the forefront of developing the ability to handle ever larger amounts of cargo.

In 2016 the terminals began to get the first glimpse of the changes which are coming. In the first half of the year, the amount of containers handled in the main ports grew more slowly than the number of containers moved globally. Naturally each container which is transported must be handled both at the export and the import location. The only explanation is therefore that we have witnessed a decline in the transhipment incidence.

That such a decline should happen is perfectly logical when one considers the way the shipping lines operate. From 2010 to 2014 the most important cost parameter for the shipping lines was fuel. This resulted in slow steaming as the natural response to bring this cost under control. Following the collapse in oil prices starting late 2014, the single largest cost component for the shipping lines changed to become port and terminal expenses. Consequently, the shipping lines shifted their focus to address this element.

Apart from demanding generally lower prices, the shipping lines had another tool at their disposal. By striving to connect more port pairs directly, without the need for transhipment, they could reduce their unit costs further. This could be done in two different ways, and shipping lines used both. One was to change their own networks to incorporate more direct services. The other was to increase the amount of collaboration with competitors to swap, or acquire, slots on board competing products offering direct services. The impact on this became clear during 2016, where in the spring one example showed a service by the Ocean-3 Alliance having no less than 12 different shipping lines on board – despite the alliance only having 3 members as well as an association with Hamburg Süd.

The lead-time for port expansions are typically in the range of 2-4 years depending on the geographical locations and the extent of the expansion. In a few locations it can even be up to 10 years. This means that ports and terminals almost by definition lag behind the development by the container lines who only operate with a 1-3 year lead time on capacity.

We are therefore facing a short to medium term future wherein the capacity in ports and terminals will be growing rapidly, both as a consequence of projects in the pipeline coming to completion, and as a consequence of automation which increases the productivity of these terminals. At the same time, it can be expected that the cargo volumes going through the terminals will exhibit only very limited growth. The net result being a development to some extent mirroring that of the shipping lines in recent years where structural overcapacity will lead especially transhipment hubs to battle over insufficient cargo volumes.

A few conclusions can be made pertaining to the current situation, which also points towards the future developments.

First of all it is clear that despite the multitude of reasons which have led to the current situation, there are two key issues which are at the heart of the matter. Furthermore these two issues will also become key for the changes that are about to happen for shipping lines, cargo owner, ports and terminals alike.

One issue is the change in industrial maturity. Moving from the 2nd growth phase into the 3rd phase of maturity have caused a fundamental shift in the underlying levels of demand growth. This does not mean the market is no longer cyclical. In all likelihood the market not only is, but will continue to be, cyclical. But the cycles will now take place around a baseline of much lower growth rates. The shift from 2nd to 3rd phase was largely happening around the time of the financial crisis. The financial crisis did not cause this shift – it would have happened regardless. However, the immediate problems brought about by the financial crisis overshadowed the more fundamental shift for a while. This is partially why the industry continued to order massive amounts of capacity – matching their past behaviour.

And here we are at the core of the second main issue. All major successful shipping lines have been successful precisely because their strategies, their tactics and their entire business models were perfectly attuned to a market in the 2nd rapid growth phase. Any company who was not, was left by the wayside. But this also indicate that, at the outset, none of the carriers are naturally attuned to be successful in the new mature 3rd phase of the industry.

Before moving on with the plethora of challenges and issues which the industry needs to deal with, it is important to note that this shift from growth to maturity is a natural development which is no different than other industries. It is a shift which is always associated with challenges for incumbents and opportunities for newcomers. And herein it must be noted that this shift is independent from other external disruptive factors such as digitization and automation. The industry would need to change even if we were not facing the fourth industrial revolution.

The key challenges to be faced

With the current market situation, and the reasons hereof, in place, it is time to take a closer look at the key challenges the industry is facing. When doing this, it is important, as mentioned earlier, to distinguish between the tactical and the strategic challenges. We will touch somewhat on the tactical challenges, but it is the strategic challenges leading up to 2025 and beyond which is the primary focus.

In order to identify key challenges, the baseline must be a forecast of how the future will develop. As mentioned initially this is not a book heavy in graphs and tables, and one of the reasons is that they tend to distract from getting an overview of the general situation. Not that data is irrelevant – far from it. Any company needs to dig deep into the data to thoroughly analyse their own situation as well as quantify the anticipated consequences of their choices. Furthermore, quantitative long-term forecasts can serve as the underpinning for the context within which an industry develops.

However, if the focus is to convey an overall understanding of the dynamics, the inclusion of myriads of numbers tend to distract from the main message. Therefore, the following outlook will not be heavy in numbers, but quantified analysis was used in order to arrive at the overall understanding.

First of all, a key question is the development of supply and demand. Let us start out with the supply side of the equation first.

In the immediate future, the outlook is fairly clear. The mega-vessels which were ordered in 2014-15 will continue to be delivered in 2017-18. The structural overcapacity will continue to place a downwards pressure on the markets, and especially panamax vessels are seen to have become redundant in the wake of the expanded set of locks in the

Panama Canal. Therefore it also appears quite certain that we will continue to see high levels of scrapping.

But what will happen from 2019 and beyond?

First of all, a disproportionate share of feeder-sized vessels will be reaching the end of their life-span, with a rapid uptake in geriatric vessels to be seen from 2020. Given that the introduction of the mega-vessels warrants the use of hub-and-spoke networks, it is to be expected that we will see a surge in the ordering of feeder sized vessels. If history is any guide, we will likely also see an over-ordering of such vessels, but as the capacity of these vessels is limited, the impact on the overall global market balance will be limited.

Secondly, the question arises as to whether we will see another round of ordering of mega vessels, whether we will see a new generation of 25.000 TEU vessels, or whether we will revert to slightly smaller vessels. This particular question is dealt with in detail in the chapter pertaining to the complexities of network design, where vessel sizes are closely linked to the development of the global sourcing patterns. The short answer for now is that we will likely see a reversal to slightly smaller deep-sea vessels.

But whereas the question pertaining to vessel sizes is one aspect to capacity, the more fundamental question is how much capacity we would expect to be ordered, and what dynamics the shipping lines should expect in this regard.

As for the amount of capacity, this will be partially guided by the expectation related to demand growth, and will be covered shortly. The dynamics of ordering will be changing compared to the past though. In the run-up to the financial crisis, as well as during the round of ordering for the 18-20.000 TEU class of vessels there was essentially 20 global shipping lines potentially contemplating ordering such vessels. The majority subsequently went ahead and placed such orders.

With the recent round of consolidation, however, this has changed. Provided all announcements as of January 2017 will be approved by the relevant competition authorities, only 8-10 shipping lines will realistically even contemplate ordering more mega-vessels. This reduces the risk of a run-away ordering process as the one seen in the wake of the Triple-E orders placed by Maersk Line in 2011.

If we then look at the amount of capacity to be ordered, this is driven by two factors. One is the anticipated demand growth, and the other is the need for replenishment capacity as older vessels are scrapped.

The current container fleet remains relatively young, but over the course of the next decade we will gradually see larger vessels become scrapped. By 2025 it will become increasingly normal to scrap vessels in the size range of 6-8.000 TEU, and half a decade after that it will become the 10.000 TEU vessels. Consequently the ordering pattern for the container shipping industry will gradually begin to resemble other, older, shipping sectors where it is common to have organic replacement of all vessel sizes. This also indicates a timeframe for when we might expect any "quantum leaps" in terms of advanced automation in the larger container shipping vessels.

In terms of demand developments, there is a confluence of different factors which will impact the industry – developments which are increasingly termed the fourth industrial revolution. Before we begin to address these topics, however, we need to contemplate the shift into industry maturity as highlighted in the past chapter.

In the industry it has for decades been a rule of thumb that container shipping demand grew three times faster than GDP. All significant analysis performed to verify this rule of thumb has largely failed, as the volatility the numbers exhibit are of such a magnitude, that any stringent correlation disappears. Container demand volumes are equally impacted by changes in inventory, shifts in sourcing patters, changes in the size of the trade goods themselves etc. etc. Nonetheless, as an average consideration the rule of thumb is not far off the mark. At heart, it simply means that there has been a multiplier between global economic growth and container growth. However, as outlined in the past chapter, the underlying growth dynamic has come to its logical conclusion – and realistically this means there is no rational basis upon which to assume container demand will exhibit growth rates materially different from the underlying economic growth itself.

It can be debated – and it certainly is being debated – whether this underlying structural growth in container demand is best described by GDP, by merchandized trade growth or by any other of a wide range of economic indicators. But irrespective of the choice of economic foundation one chooses, it does not materially change the long term outlook. The shift from the growth phase in the industry to the mature phase in itself results in a shift from 8% annual demand growth to a future of 2-4% annual demand growth over the next 10 years – of course with cyclicality around this level.

Whether the correct number is 2% or 4% largely depends on the assumptions one choose to imbue the models with, partially pertaining to the underlying global economic growth, partially pertaining to whether one believes the structural factor linking container demand to economic parameter will disappear entirely or not.

However, this outlook is the baseline given the natural development of the industry itself. On top of this, the global economy is facing major changes over the coming decade and beyond. Increasingly these changes are being termed the fourth industrial revolution and, depending on perspective, a great multitude of effects can be read into this headline. In the following we will take a closer look at the elements which will be presenting specific challenges to the container shipping industry, and subsequent chapters will take a deeper look not only at the ramifications but also what possible courses of action the shipping lines and other industry stakeholders can take.

What is meant by the term "fourth industrial revolution"? In essence, it is an abstraction and a range of definitions have been provided in recent years. The first industrial revolution was about using steam power to mechanize production as well as transportation. The second industrial revolution was about harnessing electric power, creating mass production and inventing global, instant, means of communication. The third industrial revolution was about using electronics and information technology to automate production. And finally the fourth industrial revolution is about creating a fusion between the physical, digital and biological spheres.

As can be seen, the definition of the fourth industrial revolution does become somewhat of an abstraction. In reality we would likely have to wait another 100 years before we can look back in retrospect and determine whether there really was a distinction between the third and the fourth industrial revolution. But that debate is more about labelling and semantics, where the underlying reality is that we are indeed in the midst of major global changes, which will impact the shipping industry. Additionally, a range of these changes is entirely predictable at a fundamental level, although the precise quantification can of course be debated. This is also why it becomes possible – even necessary – for shipping lines to forecast and plan for their own strategic developments ranging out to 2025 and beyond.

One of the highly predictable developments is rooted in demographics. Whereas demographic changes beyond 2025 become subject to ever increasing uncertainties, there is little change that can happen to alter our view of 2025.

The latest outlook from the United Nations indicate a global population growth from 7.4 billion in 2015 to 8.5 billion in 2030. Given the nature of demographic forecasts, the projection for 2030 is quite solid with the indicated uncertainty range being between 8.4-8.6 billion people. Whilst this remains a substantial addition to the global population, it also represents a slowing down compared to past growth rates. Looking beyond this point becomes more uncertain, with the baseline view being between 9.5 and 13.3 billion people in the year 2100, with an indicated

23% likelihood that the population will peak before 2100 and go into a negative development.

In itself, a growing population is a source of growing economic activity, and ultimately of demand for shipping services. As the growth of the population is slowing down, the demographic impact is therefore also to gradually reduce underlying economic growth. Of course this purely takes the perspective of the amount of people in the world. Another impact is the development of the wealth of the people. As an increasing number of people are being lifted out of poverty and into the – consuming – middle classes, this continues to have a positive impact on the underlying growth.

But this is where the liner shipping industry needs to take pause and contemplate where this growth is happening, and how the various population groups develop. The countries which are currently driving a substantial part of the containerized demand are also the countries for which the demographic development has reached a point where the population not only grows slower than the global average, but where the population is also ageing rapidly. The applies particularly to Europe, Japan and USA. From a global perspective the number of persons aged 60 and above is expected to increase from 900 million in 2015 to 2.1 billion in 2050. Similarly, the number of persons aged 80 and above is expected to grow from 125 million in 2015 to 434 million in 2050 reach almost a billion by 2100.

As the population expansion primarily takes place outside of the current main geographical focal areas of liner shipping, this also means that we should expect the main parts of demand growth to be in trades to or from countries not currently being on the main parts of the global networks. It will mean a geographical dispersal of the consumer demand itself. Especially the emergence of what has been termed "mega cities" with upwards of 100 million people will be a major demand driver.

But as these countries see their populations grow rapidly, they will also have the opportunity to create new main manufacturing locations, which in turn would create a dispersal of the production-led part of the supply chain.

Presently the liner shipping networks have evolved essentially around an east-west axis, centered on hub and spoke networks with mega vessels between the major ports. However, in a world where both demand and manufacturing becomes increasingly dispersed, this results in a significant challenge for shipping lines. They will find themselves operating a fleet developed for a historical demand pattern that will no longer match the reality. In the long term – towards 2050 – this is less of an issue, as the vessels which will be used then, are not yet built. However for 2025, the demographic reality will be shifting, but the main part of the fleet will not be replaceable. In the later chapter on network design it will be considered how this challenge can be tackled.

Another aspect to contemplate is the impact of the ageing population. For the majority of the demographic group it must be expected that their disposable income will decline as they enter into retirement, in itself adding a negative contribution to demand growth.

Furthermore, as people age they will be very likely to spend an increasing proportion of their disposable income on intangible services such as tourism for the more affluent and healthy segment, and on healthcare services for all segments. In countries where healthcare services are partially or predominantly covered by the state, this results in increased tax burdens, indirectly acting negatively on the demand for physical goods moved by liner shipping companies.

From a demographic perspective the liner shipping industry is thus faced with three predominant challenges:

- Increasing geographical dispersal of consumption

- Increasing geographical dispersal of manufacturing

- Ageing populations shifted disposable income from physical goods to services

Whereas shipping lines could hope that the dispersal would give rise to longer sailing distances, the problem is, that the longest sailing distances presently match with the more mature trade patterns such as Asia to Europe and Asia to the US East Coast. The emergence of the new mega cities, and their associated consumption, will likely give rise to trade lanes with a shorter average sailing distance compared to the current main trades.

Another aspect of the fourth industrial revolution is the emergence of automation. In the past couple of years, the developments in for example 3-D printing has drawn an increasing number of headlines. From an industry perspective, we are at a point where some shipping lines are experimenting with 3D-printing of spare parts on board vessels. Whilst this development can certainly help in reducing operating costs for vessel owners, this cannot be said to be major revolution in itself. Rather it is a natural evolution leading to further efficiency savings.

From a larger perspective, it is another aspect of 3-D printing which have caused a level of concern for the industry. The outset is the futuristic view that we will be able to print almost anything on a 3-D printer, and hence we will no longer have any need to manufacture physical goods in far-flung locations. The implied consequence would be a collapse in demand for container shipping services.

However, the opposing view to this would be that if 3-D printing does achieve the high ambitions many people have for it, it would also imply that mass-manufacturing processes would experience an equal quantum leap in production efficiency. And hence it would still be rational to concentrate manufacturing in specific locations instead of having it dispersed to every minor city. It would, however, also imply that the need for manufacturing to take place in very large centralized locations could be challenged, in turn dispersing production to more, smaller, locations. This development would be in perfect symbiosis with the demographic development outlined before, and further underscore the challenge that shipping companies will increasingly have to adapt to a more dispersed network as opposed to the east-west centric network.

Furthermore, the mass-production variation of the 3-D printer would more correctly be described as automated factories using robots. This is a development which is already upon us, with examples of traditional manufacturing plants, previously being operated by manual labour in China, being moved back to for example the US, where production is now performed by robots.

This change does not, however, imply that the need for shipping disappears. Instead of shipping the finished products from the manufacturing plant to the outlets selling the products, there is now a need to ship the subcomponents to be used by the automated factory. But it does reduce demand, as the subcomponents might take up less physical space than the final product.

A key challenge for the shipping lines is therefore that they will experience a negative impact on demand growth as a direct consequence of the development of automated factories and assembly plants. Incidentally, this effect is part of the concern the industry has had for several years, usually called near-shoring. This is where manufacturing is shifted back towards the place of consumption. In Europe this would for example be the relocation of manufacturing from China to Turkey. Whereas the underlying demand measured in TEU remains stable, the distance over which the cargo is moved is dramatically reduced – in turn reducing the effective demand for container vessels.

The combined effects of the demographic developments as well as the impact of the fourth industrial revolution is seen to have a high likelihood of being negative. Quantifying the individual components are fraught with uncertainty, and the reality is that no-one can with certainty predict exactly how rapidly the automation will give rise to near shoring, nor how rapidly the escalating population centres in the mega cities will gain sufficient purchasing power to drive material demand flows. For the shipping lines, this means that they need to plan and prepare in the face of this uncertainty.

At best we will maintain an annual average demand growth rate out to 2025 of 2-4%. Furthermore, one could optimistically assume that the average sailing distance for the cargo remains unchanged. In that case, global demand is set to grow 20-42% overall. This in turn leaves ample opportunity for not only absorbing the current structural overcapacity, but also with the ability to build new capacity to match the new trading patterns.

But in this context it should be noted that the current level of structural overcapacity is in the range of 10-20%. An accurate measure is not feasible as it depends on whether one for example includes the ability to speed up vessels which have been absorbed by slow steaming. Additionally the current orderbook equals some 15% of the current fleet. This means we need demand to catch up to a total of 25-35% growth to match the overcapacity and the newbuilds.

If we assume annual average scrapping at a level equating 3% of the current global fleet out to 2025, this will remove 24% of the current capacity. Such a level of scrapping would be quite high in a historic context, amounting to some 600.000 TEU per year. Overall this means that in such a scenario we would still have to order new capacity matching 9%-41% of the existing fleet size.

In this context it should be noted, that even if we take the higher end of the scale, i.e. 41% capacity growth, this implies quite subdued annual growth rates. If we assume these vessels are delivered in the 7-year period from 2019-2025, it translates into a 5% annual injection of new capacity. This is less than half of the capacity growth rate the industry has been used to, but on the other hand sufficient to ensure a gradual phase-in of new improved vessel types. As a side-issue, it should be noted that such sustained low capacity growth rates will result in significant problems for the shipyards who will find it difficult to fill their orderbooks with container vessels.

But it can also be seen, that if demand does not match the upper levels of the forecast, this will quickly curb the ability of the industry to order newer replacement vessels.

Even worse is the more negative outlook. In this case the underlying demand growth is negatively impacted by the demographic shifts to an older population in combination with near-shoring driven by the automation of manufacturing plants. A realistic view at the negative scenario can see the global demand slowly stagnating over the period. This is an effect which takes time to take hold, and if we assume zero percent demand growth becomes the norm only by 2025, the cumulative demand growth between now and 2025 becomes only 15% if we set the baseline growth in 2017 as 3%. In this case the organic demand growth over the entire period would only match the injection of capacity in 2017-2018. The structural overcapacity problem would gradually be solved through the scrapping of capacity – but this alone would not leave room for any material deliveries of new vessels out to 2025.

This is where the shipping lines need to take a close look at their options. In the positive case, they can plan for a 5% annual fleet expansion. This is not very much if new mega-vessels are being contemplated. Ordering a single batch of 20.000 TEU vessels for the Asia-Europe trade will for all main carriers significantly exceed a 5% fleet expansion. This in itself points to two key developments.

One development would be to increase the rate of scrapping in order to pave the way for not only a rebalancing of supply and demand, but also to allow for the phase-in of new vessel types. The challenge with this approach is, that any additional material increase in scrapping requires vessel owners to take losses on scrapping vessels which are not yet at the end of their natural lifespan. Whilst this from an overall perspective might still be attractive to an individual carrier, they are still subject to

41

the uncertainty, that their scrapping of capacity might be counter-acted by a competitor ordering new capacity.

The other key development it implies is, that when capacity growth has to be curbed, it will favour the ordering of smaller vessel sizes. This will allow any individual carrier to order more vessels without destabilizing their own markets. Whereas large vessels has an advantage in terms unit costs when they are full, smaller vessels has the advantage of increasing the service frequency as well as the number of port-pairs which can be covered directly. As we will see in the chapter pertaining to network design, this effect is likely to be the strongest argument for the carriers to reduce the sizes of newbuildings going forward.

Hence in the positive scenario of continued 2-4% growth the shipping lines clearly have options, but it requires a different approach to ordering and fleet composition.

In the negative scenario, the carriers face a much more severe set of choices. They can choose to continue with their current fleet, and gradually over the next 3-4 years the markets will become rebalanced, as long as they abstain from increasing the sailing speed of the vessels. They could then choose to order additional vessels, permanently instituting a situation where slow steaming cannot be reversed.

They could also choose to increase the scrapping levels dramatically. Whilst this would create the opportunity to order more new vessels, it would only compound the problems related to the losses of scrapping medium-age vessels.

Adding to the problem in the negative scenario is the dispersal of cargo to more trade lanes. This will increasingly render the mega-vessel ill-suited for the de facto trade flows, and increase the reliance on transhipments. This would create an environment wherein niche carriers would see an opportunity in using smaller vessels to provide faster, direct, services. Whether this can be done at a reasonable cost level would largely depend on the fuel costs. A high fuel cost level is an advantage for the main carriers, and would dissuade smaller niche carriers from competing head-on with the mega vessels. But a low fuel price environment undermines the value of the hub and spoke setup, and opens the market for niche players using small vessels at high speeds to provide differentiated services.

Hence the demand developments present the shipping lines with an added set of key challenges:

- The injection of new capacity will at best be relatively low, preventing a quick renewal of vessels even when new, better, technology becomes available

- In the negative scenario it will become necessary to increasingly scrap medium-aged vessels at a loss

- Whilst the mega-vessels have a unit cost advantage, none of the scenarios favour further ordering of such vessel types

There are multiple keys to successfully handling the challenges brought about by the changing supply and demand environment. Whilst the execution of this will differ between different shipping lines, the overall elements will be variations over the same themes. In addition to the fleet composition and nature of newbuilding programs, they also include more structured approaches to network design as well as how to leverage additional consolidation whether through mergers or through alliances.

As previously mentioned, another aspect of the fourth industrial revolution is the fusion between the physical, digital and biological spheres. In the context of shipping it is primarily the fusion of the physical and digital sphere which is of interest. This fusion gives rise to a range of challenges which will be dealt with individually in the coming chapters. But as an overall view, this results in the following key challenges:

- How to generate value from data

- How to use automation to cut costs, drive commoditization and at the same time create a competitive advantage through differentiation. Despite the obvious contradiction in terms, this is achievable.

- How to act in an environment of complete data transparency

The value of inefficiencies

An impediment to any change, no matter how well warranted, is the value gained by individual stakeholders stemming from inefficiencies in existing business models. Furthermore, this value is often hidden within complex networks of different stakeholders.

As a simplistic outset, consider the shipment of containers between a minor port in Indonesia and a minor port in Italy. In order to facilitate this shipment we would likely see the involvement of a feeder shipping line between Indonesia and a large regional hub port, a major shipping line onwards to a hub port in the Mediterranean followed by yet another feeder line to the final minor port in Italy. Additionally, there will be the involvement of origin and destination trucking companies. Agents could be involved to assist in generating and processing the necessary documentation in terms of Bills of Lading, load manifests etc. The buyer and the seller of the cargo would have their own banks involved, generating letters of credit as well as getting freight insurance. On the shipping side, the containers might be from a leasing company, and a 3rd party service might be employed to handle inspection, maintenance and repair of the containers. Moving beyond the individual shipment, the circle of stakeholders would be expanded to also include vessel brokers, classification societies, freight forwarders, eCommerce portal providers, terminal operators, stevedores, pilots etc. A fully exhaustive list would become the basis for an entire book in itself.

Every single stakeholder fulfils a role in the supply chain of moving the container from Indonesia to Italy. Either in the context of the specific shipment, or in the context of ensuring that the shipping line has the possibility to offer the service at all.

Analysis of every individual stakeholder might well show that the task performed is performed efficiently. However, herein lies part of the problem for transforming the industry. Providing a service, no matter how efficiently it is done, also has the potential for degrading the efficiency of the overall system.

We should contemplate it in the following context. A shipping line initially handle all processes related to the shipment of a container. After a while they discover that they are not very efficient at a certain process. An intermediary company steps in and performs the specific task more efficiently. Hence a net gain to the system has been obtained. Over time – in the context of shipping quite literally over centuries – an intricate web of stakeholders each with their own niche services have evolved. It is exceedingly likely, that at the creation of each stakeholder they did improve the efficiency overall of the system.

But this also means that any new development – or invention – which would bypass an entire category of intermediaries would be met with fierce resistance. In this case is does not matter how efficient the intermediary is – if his process can be entirely eliminated, he would disappear. Clearly such intermediaries would attempt to halt any such development, or, failing that, attempt to co-opt the development to make it suit their own needs.

Hence what likely started out as value-creating enterprises will in the coming years see their roles shift. They will instead be the stewards of business propositions which are at heart based on maintaining inefficiencies in the system.

What might these inefficiencies be? If one contemplates the full supply chain multiple examples immediately appears.

One example is the role of the small NVOCC, who simply acts as an intermediary for simple transactional freight between a cargo owner and a shipping line. Originally, they provided significant value to a small cargo owner who had neither the time, nor the knowledge, to examine the market for relevant freight solutions and obtain a workable price. However going forward, as will be examined in the chapter about yield management, this will become simplified to the point where such an intermediary is no longer needed.

Another example is a booking agent acting on behalf of a cargo owner. An entire industry has appeared over the past 15 years where the shipping lines' drive towards the use of electronic bookings and shipping instructions has forced an increasing amount of cargo owners to interact electronically with the shipping line. A range of cargo owners have not had the inclination to automate their own internal supply chain processes, and hence found themselves unable, or unwilling, to comply with the electronic requirements. An intermediary solution has subsequently developed whereby the cargo owner continues with his old processes, and the booking agent bridges the gap to the eCommerce systems. In this situation very little value is added to the overall system, and whereas the shipping line will see it as an improvement, the cargo owner will see it as an added cost.

A final example is the range of companies who offer to verify invoices issued by shipping lines. The invoicing accuracy from many shipping lines is so poor, that a cargo owner will find value in this process. Whereas solid statistics are not available, it has been indicated that in 2015 approximately 20-30% of all invoices had some levels of error. This is a clear case of a business model – for the verifying companies – which is entirely predicated on the inefficiencies inherent in the industry.

As we move forward into an era of automation and transparency, many intermediaries will find their business models to be either eroded or eliminated.

The Nature of Business Relations

When the changes in the industry over the next decade are contemplated, the starting point is not only in terms of which new "inventions" might we see, and how they will change the world. In other words, change is not only linked to the ramifications of the fourth industrial revolution. Some of the more fundamental changes are rooted in much more simple problems which, despite their simplicity, has been dogging the industry for years.

A key aspect in this context is the nature of business relations between the shipping lines and their customers. In essence the problem is the perceived lack of adherence to agreements and is a matter which has been brought up consistently in all major liner shipping conferences for the last couple of decades.

In theory it appears to be an easy problem to solve. You enter into a signed contract, and both parties adhere to the contract. In practice the industry is far from this level of simplicity.

The approach from shipping lines and shippers also differ in terms of their view on the obligation to adhere to such contracts. Before we examine how the nature of these business relations are likely to change over the coming years, let us first take a closer look at the nature of the problem, and how it has been compounding over the years.

Let us start with examining a shipper and shipping line who enter into what appears to be a straightforward contract. The contract stipulates that the shipper will commit to booking 10 forty-foot containers per week for the next 10 weeks from Hong Kong to Rotterdam. The shipping line commits to transporting these containers at a freight rate of 1000 USD plus a variable fuel surcharge depending on developments in the oil price.

Even if both parties enter into this agreement in good faith, a plethora of things might happen.

As a starting point, the factory may have an problem resulting in production being delayed. The shipper might, for example, have purchased the goods ex-works and is not responsible for, or in control of, the facture production schedule. The shipper might be informed of this only shortly before the cargo was supposed to be picked up. In this case the shipper cannot fulfil his part of the agreement – yet he might request the booking of 20 containers the following week to meet his own overall delivery schedule.

For the shipping line this is problematic as it is likely not possible to find replacement cargo at the last moment. The net result being a vessel with 10 empty slots and a resultant loss in revenue. Given the industry practice, there is often no possibility to get the shipper to pay a cancellation fee.

As this continues to happen across multiple shippers, the shipping line gradually increases the amount of overbookings in order to ensure a high vessel utilization even in the face of such last minute downfall.

The next logical development is, that in some weeks downfall is less than expected. This results in the shipping line having too much cargo for the vessel, being forced to leave some containers behind. For the carrier there is no penalty associated with leaving cargo behind, they merely need to inform the shipper that this is what has happened.

For the shipper it disrupts the supply chain and is highly undesirable. As this continues to happen, the shipper takes two precautions. One is to build a buffer into the supply chain, which adds overall cost – a cost they de facto will seek to get compensated for through lower freight rates. The second is to indicate a larger amount of containers to be booked than they genuinely expect. This is in an attempt to insulate themselves against their cargo being left behind.

But these developments only result in a higher incidence of cargo not showing up, and now at even lower freight rates. The shipping line responds by increasing overbookings and a vicious cycle is born. Depending on geography, the amount of downfall can today range as high as 40%.

The above simplistic outline only captures a minor part of the problem related to the business relationship. Compounding the effect are issues relating to the available of the containers themselves – it does a shipper no good to have space on the vessel, but then being told there are no more empty containers available for pick-up in the depot.

Furthermore the above outline is in a situation where neither party make their decisions based on a desire to take unfair advantage of each other. However, such behaviour is also endemic amongst some shippers and shipping lines.

Some shippers will enter into a freight agreement knowing they will never deliver the promised freight volumes. Some shipping lines will deliberately overbook to the point where they are certain of cargo overflow, and hence cargo being left behind. Both types of behaviour have a positive short-term business case associated with them.

The shipper will be able to obtain lower freight rates as well as the opportunity to play an arbitrage game between the contract market and the spot market.

The shipping line will improve vessel utilization and hence reduce their unit costs.

This type of behaviour tends to reinforce itself. Once one of the parties feel themselves to be aggrieved, they will tend to counter-act this, fuelling a downwards spiral. The mere fact that this dynamic has been a major talking point at liner shipping conferences for the past 20 years, yet the situation has only deteriorated, speaks volumes as to the difficulty of changing this within the confines of the existing business models.

Only one major case exist where a minor shipping line, in the wake of its bankruptcy, filed a lawsuit against the shippers for failing to deliver the volumes as agreed, and hence demanding that penalties should be paid as per contract. The case took place on the Transpacific and the suit was filed with the court in New York in 2011. The case was ruled upon by the court in spring 2016, and the ruling was largely in favour of the shippers. The case is currently under appeal by the curators of the shipping line, but for now it is not only business practice that there are no repercussions for not adhering to contract, it is – to some degree – now also legally entrenched.

Compounding the problems are the contractual agreements pertaining to for example free time, equipment availability and equipment substitution as well as surcharges.

In some cases these are easily enforced, but in other cases business practices prevent their effective implementation and serves to further undermine the business relationship.

But this is the problem for now. How will this change towards 2025?

Key drivers of changing contract relationships

Given the past developments it is unrealistic to expect a sudden mindset shift resulting in all parties adhering to contracts. Something else will have to happen.

Several developments are underway to support the notion of such a change, and all of them are linked to different ways of pricing and contracting.

One aspect is the gradual development of online freight platforms for spot cargo. As spot rates become instantly visible, allowing shippers to book directly, this might in the short term act to further result in non-performance of the contracts. A shipper with a contract at a freight rate of 1000 USD will be strongly tempted to renege on the agreement if he can easily book passage on the same trade lane at 500 USD. Even more tempting if the online rate is available from a shipping line who is a member of the same alliance as the one with which he holds the contract. In this case the cargo will even move on the exact same ship, but at a considerable discount. Over the coming decade we will see an emergence of a multitude of online freight portals – more likely driven by small and medium sized NVOCCs in the initial phases – and hence the temptation for shippers to switch to such products in periods of overcapacity - and associated low rates - will increase.

The second development is in the realm of new contract types. The approach to these is parallel to the development the airline industry experienced some 40 years ago. Back then it was often possible to cancel a flight ticket at the last moment at no added cost to the passenger – a problem similar to the one faced today by the shipping lines. The airlines solved the problem by introducing a new contract type. It was a flight ticket which was priced differently, had to be paid up-front, and which could not be cancelled. Existing customers were told they could choose between the two, and hence there was not the need to force customers to accept new cancellation terms. Over time the price difference meant that the majority of customers switched to the new contract type, dramatically improving the predictability of cargo flow - in the sense that passengers are to be equated with cargo.

For the container shipping markets new contract types are being tested in the market which are neither spot cargo nor traditional contract cargo. They are a variation over the same model as successfully implemented by the airlines and provides shippers and shipping lines the opportunity to choose either the old or the new types of contracts. The new contracts require shippers to place a certain minimum of collateral, though not pay for the full freight up front as was the case for the airlines. In the case of non-delivery of the promised bookings, the shipper will pay a penalty secured against the collateral. Conversely, if the shipping line fails to ship the cargo as agreed, they will have to pay a penalty to the shipper. Pilot tests thus far indicate that this contract type results in a substantial reduction in the amount of non-conformances versus standard contracts.

The third development is in the realm of service standards. Part of the problem in the industry has been measuring whether either party delivered what they were supposed to. One service aspect is the simple operational quality – basically whether the container was delivered on time as agreed. The problem is that if a container is delivered too late, it can be caused by many factors. The shipping line might have overbooked and left the cargo behind, in which case the service failure is the shipping line's fault. The shipper might have submitted incomplete shipping instructions preventing the shipping line from legally loading the container on board the vessel, in which case the service failure is the shipper's fault. A typhoon might have delayed the cargo in which case the service failure is due to force majeure. Presently the poor data quality and haphazard back-end IT infrastructure prevents many shipping lines from providing a solid end-to-end view of the quality of the service provided as well as the reasons hereof.

However, with the development of new and better IT systems, combined with Big Data analytical capabilities, the automation of such service quality measurements will become standard over the coming decade. This has the implication that it also becomes simple to build service measures into contracts and automatically verify whether services has been delivered as agreed.

If we combine these developments, it is clear that the shipping lines face a range of choices, all of which are aimed at improving the business relationships and contract adherence.

First of all it would seem as if there is a choice in whether to show freight rates online. However, in reality this is not a choice. Over time we will see an increasing number of online NVOCCs – either pure online companies with no pre-history in liner shipping, or existing NVOCCs who see this as a way to increase their sales and marketing potential. These will provide transparent pricing to anyone who accesses their sites.

The shipping lines could of course choose not to follow suit. In cases where the online NVOCCs show prices which are not markedly below the rates of the shipping lines themselves, this would be less of an issue. However, when online rates go significantly below contract rates, the problem for the shipping lines appear.

Shipping lines could choose a countermove whereby they do not offer attractive rates to such online NVOCCs, however this does not prevent aggressive online pricing. For an online NVOCC who might see his revenue stream stem from the sales of other related services online, they might be perfectly willing to display below-cost ocean rates online. And of course re-selling of slots amongst NVOCCs could also undermine attempts to prevent them from posting online rates.

Therefore, the choice the shipping lines is facing is one of *how* rates should be handled online, not *whether* they should be online. The manner in which this choice is made will be a determining factor in transforming the business relationship. Several options are available, depending on the value proposition of the shipping line.

Spot relations

First it should be clear for the shipping lines that it will not be possible to have differentiated freight rates for different customers as far as the online rates are concerned. The transparency in itself will prevent such a differentiation. Price differences can be maintained for different product types – such as different equipment types provided, but any non-warranted price differential will be the subject of arbitrage in a transparent rate environment.

This in turn also leads to the conclusion that online rates will be predominantly for spot cargo for the smaller shippers. As the IT infrastructure develops further, it becomes possible to link ocean transport with land based transport, ultimately resulting in the possibility for even smaller cargo owners to purchase transactional freight products from door to door.

In such an environment it is in the interest of the shipping lines to actively develop a strategy to handle this. Otherwise, as already mentioned, this part of the market will become controlled by online NVOCCs and online forwarders.

We are currently seeing a rapid development in the space for either providing or facilitating online container freight, with substantial investments having been made in this sector in 2016. These ventures are mainly driven by a combination of people with a background in other disruptive IT platform products and people with a background in shipping for forwarding services.

Some existing large NVOCCs and freight forwarders are also actively developing tools or platforms of their own to support this development. However, from a practical standpoint, the shift to online, transparent, freight for the simple shipments will ultimately serve to undermine margins for this specific part of the market. As such it is not in the short-term interest of major NVOCCs to support such a development, however they need to prepare themselves to join the development once it gains momentum.

For the shipping lines, this presents an opportunity to regain business relations directly with the smaller cargo owners. This is a segment of customers which the shipping lines have gradually lost control over in the past 20 years. In general, the major shipping lines have become increasingly difficult to do business with for small cargo owners resulting in a situation where freight forwarders have stepped into the gap and provided the necessary support. Regaining the ability to price directly towards this segment is a significant opportunity to not only aim at eliminating some of the forwarder controlled business, but also to pursue a much more active pricing strategy aimed at not only improving freight rates, but also at using more advanced tools for pricing discovery and yield management. This is in itself a significant area of change and will be considered further in the chapter about Yield Management.

Finally, in order for online spot rates to work, it becomes necessary to make the spot bookings enforceable as well. If online spot bookings are not enforceable, there is nothing preventing a predatory booking strategy whereby all online rates are automatically monitored, and every time a slightly lower rate is available a new booking is made while cancelling the old booking.

Whereas it might appear appealing to immediately introduce full freight payment at time of booking, this is not likely to succeed in the short term. Instead the development can be supported by a gradual development as follows.

Initially, shippers intent on booking at spot prices will be required to pay a booking fee at the time of booking. In case of a cancellation, the booking fee will be forfeited. Given that this all takes place in an online environment, this requires the shipping lines to develop facilities for online payments of such booking fees.

The next step would be to allow the spot shipper a choice between paying the booking fee upfront or paying the full freight upfront – with a price difference between the two products. The full freight option basically matching what is seen for a non-refundable airline ticket. This approach will gradually mature the spot market to the point where cargo owner in need of spot shipments can choose the spot product based on how certain they are of the cargo materializing.

The final step would be for the shipping lines to have a credit evaluation process, whereby spot customers who have been granted credit terms will be allowed to book without the payment of the upfront booking fee, but will be subject to paying any subsequent cancellation fees.

Contract relations

For larger shippers, the markets will gradually evolve towards enforceable contracts – simply because shipping lines need to create a higher degree of predictability of their cargo flows, and shippers similarly need predictability for their own supply chains. The question is therefore how this development will unfold itself, not whether contracts will become more enforceable.

The contract market for larger shippers is different from the spot shipments, as the requirements from the shippers are markedly different.

In this case it not only due to substantially larger volumes being shipped – which in itself results in negotiations over volume discounts – but particularly due to the need for regularity in the supply chain. Regularity means that the shipper needs a steady flow of cargo on specific trade corridors, they need to be assured that empty containers are available at the origin locations, they need a stable freight rate for their own planning purposes and they need a certain level of customer service to assist when problems occur with the shipments.

As mentioned earlier, the state of affairs today is that many contracts are not being adhered to – neither by the shipper nor by the shipping lines. Note that does not mean all contracts are not adhered to. Clearly some relationships do honour the contracts, but these are increasingly not the norm.

What we will see develop is a market for enforceable contracts where both shipper and shipping line are willing to commit to the terms of the contract to the point of incurring penalties for non-conformance. Just as seen with the airline tickets, it is a much more likely approach to see such enforceable contracts introduced as a separate product in the market, than try to force all existing contractual relationships into a new form.

An enforceable contract will stipulate the shipment of certain volumes at agreed prices for time periods likely stretching up to 12 months into the future. Realistically, enforceable contracts will be unlikely to see durations exceed 12 months. The reason for this is two-fold. Partly because the cargo owner regularly needs to change his supply-chain setup. Locking into enforceable contracts for a period beyond 12 months would reduce his market agility. Partly because the shipping lines have a need to regularly adjust their shipping networks. Whilst minor network adjustments tend to happen quite frequently, any major network adjustments tend to take place on an annual scale – typically coinciding with the seasonal market slump after Chinese New Year.

The enforceable contract will change the relationship between the shipper and the shipping line. Early tests of some enforceable contracts show a much higher degree of predictability than existing contracts. The value of this is further explored in the chapter concerning Yield Management.

This allows the shipper and shipping line to shift focus away from negotiations over non-adherence to contract in relation to downfalls or cargo rolling, and onto service level parameters such as reliability, timeliness of documentation and supply chain visibility.

Additionally, enforceable contracts allows the introduction of trade financing. This involves a 3rd party, such as a bank, to step in and manage the credit and payment process. In order for this to apply, the individual cargo owners would need to establish a credit rating and relationship with the bank offering the trade financing. In these cases, the net result could be that the shipper is offered a certain amount of credit days by the bank – potentially at credit terms which are more favourable than those offered by the shipping line, whereas the shipping line might get paid in full at the time of booking.

Whereas the online spot rates by definition need to be open and transparent for all to see, the market for enforceable contracts will likely develop in two parallel tracks. One part of the development will see an open and transparent market for the booking of freight on contract at least 12 months into the future. This makes the market both transparent and efficient for small and medium sized shippers who prioritize stability higher than the ability to try to outsmart the spot market.

Another part of the development pertains to enforceable contracts for larger shippers who will be negotiating individual agreements with the shipping lines. The terms and conditions for these large agreements might differ from the standard terms offered by the shipping lines, but in order to have an efficient execution of the agreements, it is beneficial to use the enforceable contract framework. Not only does it reinforce the mutual commitment, it also allows shipping lines to have a streamlined internal process for handling contracts and thus ensuring a much less error-prone approach to making invoices.

Finally, the creation of enforceable contracts with the largest shippers also allows these shippers to use the online spot market at the same time, whilst at all times making it clear – and automated – which bookings are contractual and which are spot.

Hybrid between spot and contract

When the online spot market as well as the market for enforceable contracts are both well established, this allows shippers to develop their own hybrid use between the two. A shipper might choose to engage into enforceable contracts for major cargo volumes on stable port-port corridors, which choosing to use the online spot market for smaller, more infrequent, shipments. In order for this hybrid to work, it is of course crucial that both contract types are binding, as otherwise we will continue to see some market participants leverage spot rates against contract rates depending on whether the market is weak or strong.

Action Point: Enforceability

In conclusion, there is one single word that will come to characterize the development in the relationship between shippers and shipping lines, and that is "enforceability".

Enforceability is the key to improving predictability in the supply chain for both shippers and shipping lines.

Enforceability is the key to improving yield management and vessel utilization for the shipping lines

Enforceability is the key for the shippers to improve stability in the supply chain, while at the same time being able to use an effective online spot market

Enforceability is the key for shipping lines to develop differentiated products in the market and get them priced accordingly

Enforceability is an absolute necessity to automate business processes and successfully drive digitization in the supply chain

Key questions for exploration for both shipping lines and cargo owners:

What is the value of a certain percentage of increase in contract enforceability versus your current business performance?

How do you plan to create enforceability?

How do you plan to define which types of exceptions gives rise to an allowable deviation from the agreement?

Exception Management at the Core

Today most shipping lines see their core business as moving cargo from origin to destination. Some shipping lines have quite simple products, mainly related to the ocean transportation. Others have more extended transportation products involving land side transportation as well as logistics and supply chain management services. Hence how they define their core business will tend to differ, but fundamentally it is related to moving cargo from one point to another.

The problem for many liner shipping companies is that in addition to the growth rates being reduced as a consequence of the market maturing, a significant part of the market is becoming commoditized, and this will increasingly be the case as we move towards 2025.

That the market is commoditized is an aspect which continues to be challenged, especially by some shipping lines. Therefore, it is important to take a closer look at what commoditization means, why it will increase in the coming decade – and how the shipping lines need to change their fundamental view on the value they offer to the customers in order to develop differentiated products.

Is the market commoditized?

Simply put, a commodity is a product which is easily interchanged with a similar product from a different producer or vendor. Note that almost no commodities in the world are 100% interchangeable even though they are clearly commodities in commoditized markets.

An example would be the market for crude oil. The oil market is highly commoditized, yet the reality is that different oilfields produce oil with quite different chemical compositions. Some are high in Sulphur content, some are extremely viscous and some have a high proportion of lighter hydrocarbons. Yet despite these actual differences, crude oil is essentially seen as being commoditized. There are standard price indices for crude oil in general, but the actual price for oil from a specific oilfield will be offset from the index to reflect either a higher or a lower price. But despite the factual differences in product quality, the market dynamics are those of a commoditized market.

For liner shipping we are increasingly seeing the same development. The commoditization is, however, not global in nature. Some trade corridors remain the prerogative of local niche service providers and cannot be said to be commoditized. However, for the main trade lanes, such as Asia to Europe and Asia to North America this is increasingly the case.

At this point it must be made clear that the commoditization is principally focused on the ocean part of the transportation – i.e. the ability to make an empty standard container available to a shipper, and subsequently ship this standard container from one port location to another.

Shipping lines do tend to differentiate in their ability to provide inland transportation, the levels of service they can assist with in terms of for example documentation and availability of specialized equipment. These are all differentiated elements, but to be seen in the same light as the different chemical compositions in crude oil. They provide for an offset, positive or negative, versus the underlying commoditized market but are not seen as fundamentally different products.

The shipping lines have, through the increased reliance on alliances, themselves created the commoditized market environment. An alliance of 6 shipping lines will be definition all provide the exact same physical port to port product. From a product perspective, the base product is the same, but the 6 shipping lines will differ on the service levels surrounding this core product. Some shippers have indeed used this as part of their negotiation strategies whereby they have identified an alliance they would like to use, but play the alliance members against each other on price. For these shippers the product is therefore seen as a commodity.

The extreme volatility seen in both spot and contract markets in the main deep-sea trades also indicate the presence of a commoditized market. A significant proportion of shippers are clearly willing to shift their cargo between shipping lines depending on who offers the best price – possibly plus or minus the offset an auxiliary service level might warrant. This in turn clearly indicate that these shippers see the core port to port product as a commodity.

With the market on the cusp of shifting from four to three alliances on the main deep-sea trades, the commoditization will be given added momentum.

Some shipping lines have actively worked on fighting, or reversing, this drive towards commoditization. But as can be seen, the physical reality on the deep-sea trades is that the core products are indeed becoming commoditized. The argument then typically centres around the service levels being the differentiator to prevent commoditization. Service levels can indeed be a source of price differentiation – just as crude oil with a low Sulphur content can command a certain premium versus a crude oil with a high Sulphur content.

With the magnitude, and diversity, of the fleets controlled by the major container shipping lines it is highly unlikely that any will be able to develop a physical product which is materially different from the competitors on the alliance controlled deep-sea trades. As cargo volumes, vessel sizes and the number of weekly services increase on secondary trades, these will gradually also be commoditized in the sense that the major shipping lines are unable to make truly different products.

Looking towards 2025, the commoditization will become even more pronounced. As we shall see in the coming chapters, process management and automation will be strong forces in the coming decade. But as processes are streamlined, and ultimately automated, many service elements also become commoditized. If shipping lines are successful in automating and digitizing all documentation, from sales to booking to Bill of Lading to invoicing and payment, this also means that differentiation on these service elements disappear. As either shipping lines or freight forwarders integrate their processes and systems with land-based transportation providers, differentiation on this element is also reduced.

In itself, this does not appear to be a viable future for the shipping lines, and as such it is understandable that strong forces remain trying to counter-act commoditization. However, it is equally clear that the combination of alliances, larger vessels, process management, digitization and automation will provide a strong force in ensuring the commoditization of significant parts of the market.

The strategic opportunity for the shipping lines lies elsewhere. It only requires a single major shipping line to succeed with digitization and automation in order to accelerate the commoditization. Any shipping line which is able to digitize and automate will create a significant cost advantage, and other lines will either have to follow suit or ultimately leave the market due to high internal costs.

This is where the flip-side of automation comes to the forefront. When automation is being discussed, it is usually from the perspective of the efficiencies it will create, and there is indeed a separate chapter on this later.

But the shipping industry is a physical industry. It is physical in the sense that large steel vessels sail thousands of miles on the oceans. It is physical in the sense that billions of tons of cargo are lifted on and off the ships while they are at port. In such an environment, exceptions will always occur no matter how well-planned and executed the automation is.

There will be adverse weather conditions forcing significant deviations from schedule, and at times causes loss of cargo or worse. There will be mechanical break-down of crane and equipment in the ports delaying cargo handling. Trucks carrying the containers become entangled in traffic accidents, damaging goods. Theft causes cargo to disappear en route. Physical mishaps will continue to be a part of the supply chain. Better process control and automation can reduce the incidence somewhat but not eliminate it.

This means that the path to commercial success in the commoditized market lies principally in how exceptions are handled. In this context, it is assumed that the shipping lines are capable of competent and comprehensive automation and process management over the coming decade, and therefore the baseline is a market wherein the shipping lines have indeed managed to automate all major functions. Shipping lines who have not managed to do this by 2025 are not likely to remain as major shipping lines.

Automation means that whenever the shipment proceeds according to plan there is no manual intervention. However, when there is a deviation from plan, this is where the shipping line can create a truly differentiated service.

First of all the shipping line needs to create automated routines which not only detects deviation from plan, but which can also predict when deviations from plan are likely to occur. A simply example would of course be the integration of weather reports and operational systems to predict a future delay in cargo delivery. Another example would be integration of global news sources to predict disruptions to cargo flows related to local strikes. A more sophisticated example would be the use of accelerometers build into remote tracking devices on the container to predict possible cargo damage due to rough handling.

However, reporting on service disruptions – whether at the time or predicting them ahead of time – will also be an expected service in a digitized environment. The key is lies in answering the most important question: What are you going to do about it?

Whereas the handling of some types of service failures might be automatable, often these will be incidents that local customer service staff will need to handle. This in turn will change the way shipping lines need to organize, and train, staff at their local agencies.

Today a significant amount of time for customer staff is spent handling elements of the shipment process which is actually proceeding according to plan. This can be providing booking confirmations upon checking vessel and equipment availability. It can be issuance of Bills of Lading. It can follow-up on invoicing disputes or trying to locate equipment which has not been returned as well as a plethora of other vital tasks. Some of these processes are being handled by customer service staff in the country where the shipment is taking place, others have been outsourced to major service centers typically located in India, China or the Philippines.

Once the digitization transformation is completed, essentially all of these tasks will have become automated. Shipping lines will have much reduced need for customer staff in handling these tasks. Instead they will need to have a highly competent local customer service workforce whose primary task will be to assist customers with their supply chain once things no longer proceed according to plan.

This has three major ramifications for the staffing of local agencies. One consequence is that the staff will need to have a very high skill level in devising impromptu solutions. Their ability to work with local authorities, trucking companies, ports, depots, air cargo providers, rail companies etc. will be a crucial part of their ability to assist in correcting the supply chain for the customer.

From a training perspective this will be uniquely challenging going forward. Today, customer service representatives will have been spending significant amounts of time handling the standard process, and then when they need to find a solution for an exception they are already highly familiar with the inner workings of the supply chain. In the future, a new employee coming into an agency will no longer be exposed to the inner workings of the normal process, as much of this will have become automated. In other words, they will be called upon to find solutions to complex problems without having the natural understanding of the simple problems.

One way of accomplishing this would be to create a continuous training program based on local customer service staff working in simulated training environments in order for them to get a hands-on understanding of the core elements of the process.

The second consequence is the need to provide a significant degree of decision making authority to the local organizations. In a digitized – and transparent – environment, the shipper will instantly know when his supply chain has been disrupted. A shipping line who has a solid model for forecasting service failures might have some advance warning of this before the shipper. But either way, the customer service staff who needs to handle this problem will have a relatively short window within which to devise an alternate plan. Being responsive in this situation becomes a major competitive advantage. In order for this to succeed, it requires agencies to have a significant level of decision making power in order to arrange alternate solutions quickly.

Today the level of decision making power placed in the local agencies differ significantly across shipping lines, and this will give shipping lines who are used to having local decision making power an advantage in turning exception handling into a competitive differentiator.

The third consequence will be a shift away from centralized global service centers and towards local agencies. Whereas the standardized processes for the supply chain are well suited for placement in global service centers, the handling of exceptions are particularly ill suited for such a placement.

On the positive side, the creation of a few centralized customer service desks to handle exceptions allows for a concentration, and wider usage, of highly skilled customer service representatives. However, this approach is undermined by the resultant lack of detailed local knowledge. When the supply chain gets disrupted, the solution needed to alleviate the problem will often involve the usage of local resources. In this case skilled service staff situated locally are more likely to be able to identify the best possible solutions for the specific exception.

Additionally, there is the element of conveying a sense of competence to the shippers. As long as the cargo moves according to plan, a cargo owner might be perfectly happy to use only online tools provided to him, or potentially call a global service center with a question. However, once the cargo no longer moves according to plan this is likely to become a major problem for him. A carrier which is able to quickly provide him with an alternate solution and a local contact point who takes charge of managing the alternate solution is a significant competitive differentiator.

Action Point: Exception Management

Looking towards 2025, this means that shipping lines need to acknowledge that the ocean transportation will become increasingly commoditized, and the ability to differentiate on basic transportation will quickly diminish as digitization and automation takes hold.

However, it is also clear that due to the physical nature of the industry, shipping lines have the ability to shift the competitive focus from the movement of all cargo to the handling of cargo which is subjected to exceptions. Such a shift also serves to shift the competitive focus away from something that is relatively easy to replicate once it has been automated, to an area which requires highly skilled people and the ability to manage a global organization with a high degree of local autonomy.

Key questions for exploration for an individual company:

How do you plan to predict exceptions in the supply chain?

How do you plan to use exception management as a competitive differentiator?

How do you plan to train customer service staff differently in the future?

How to you plan to organize and empower local agencies in the future?

Process Management and Control

With the significant focus being levied on digitization and automation, it is concerning that very limited focus is awarded to process management. Essentially, digitization and automation cannot take place in an environment where there is limited process management – and in some cases even limited process awareness.

From a very practical standpoint, automation requires well-defined process which can be turned into computer code. The less defined the process is, the more likely it is that the program will not perform as expected causing more problems than it solves.

And from an equally practical standpoint, digitization requires data. If processes are not well defined, this results in poor data quality. Partly because incomplete data is accepted and partly because some input data is regularly ignored in favour of other action.

This is why the chapter on process management and control has been placed before any chapters on digitization and automation – from the perspective of any shipping line, or other industry stakeholder, processes must be clearly managed prior to any full-fledged digitization and automation.

The challenge with this topic is that basically any shipping line will – correctly in their view – claim that they certainly have their processes well defined and under control. They will all be able to produce thousands of pages of Standard Operating Procedures and checklists related to anything from vessel bunkering to credit scoring of customers to safety guidelines in the case of fire in the office.

Additionally, all major shipping lines have a variety of eCommerce tools allowing for electronic bookings, shipping instructions, track and trace, schedules etc. Surely the presence of such tools also signal that there are underlying standard processes.

But this is not what is meant by process management. Process management is an entire discipline in itself, and has been used through a substantial range of industries for decades. Most well known in the form of LEAN management.

Essentially process management is not about creating a myriad of SOPs. Process management is about creating a well-defined workflow which has a predictable outcome. The outcome should be the same irrespective of who carries it out. Furthermore, the predictability should be used to continuously improve the workflow. As the outcome is predictable it is possible to quantify and measure the impact of a change and then conclude whether the change was advantageous or not.

There are a number of different ways, differing slightly in the tools and language used, in which to implement process management. But in essence it is comprised of a sequence of elements.

Initially the existing processes are mapped, and the outcome of the processes are quantified and measured. Once this baseline is established, improvements are first planned in terms of process changes, a pilot test of the improvement is carried out, the effects of the pilot are measured and if they confirm the initial expectation the improvement is fully implemented.

Whilst being simple in principle, the actual implementation of process management in shipping lines have been fraught with difficulties for a number of – good and bad – reasons.

One reason is that even though a shipping line might believe they have standard processes, it often turns out that many processes differ significantly from country to country. This is mainly due to four key reasons: Different trade practices in different countries, Different legislative environments, Ingrained internal work habits and division of decision making authority between global, regional and local entities.

However, even though legislation might indeed differ between countries, this does not preclude the development and implementation of standardized workflows which can then cater for exceptions brought about by local legislation.

As for trade practices this becomes slightly more challenging, and the most important stakeholder in this context is the customer. Due to the competitive pressure, it has over the years been opportune for the shipping lines to offer larger customers individual standard operating procedures matching the customers' needs. In some cases, this is also provided to small and medium sized customers. From a customer-focused perspective this appears sensible, as it allows a carrier to differentiate its service offering, in turn getting a higher freight rate, a larger market share or at least a more loyal customer.

This approach worked well for smaller shipping lines, but as they bigger lines grew exponentially over the past few decades, this approach becomes unmanageable. It is not feasible to have 100.000 customers out of which maybe 40.000 are given some kind of special treatment outside a normal process.

Introducing process management in this context is not about eliminating all possibilities to differentiate services, however it is about defining exactly which different services are available and ensuring the organization is capable of delivering in a cost efficient manner.

In terms of the ingrained internal work processes this is a major barrier to overcome to introduce process management – not just for shipping lines but in general. This in turn means that in order for shipping lines to effectively introduce process management they must at the same time demonstrate a willingness to ensure compliance with the new processes.

When such adherence to process management is implemented, the key risk is, that this might conflict with the need for local staff to assist customers in handling exception as outlined in the previous chapter. The change to process management must therefore be planned and executed in a carefully planned and deliberate manner taking the human resource aspect into account as well.

This partly overlaps with the fourth aspect, namely the division of decision making authority between the global, regional and local offices. Process compliance is not something only applicable to the local offices, it applies throughout the organization.

In order for a shipping line to fully control and optimize their processes, this will have to be anchored at the very top of the organization. Examples have been seen wherein shipping lines have for example stated that everything under the control of the COO could begin a transformation to process management, whereas this transformation process was not allowed to interfere with the CCO as "his" portfolio was not going to change into process management.

Such an approach might conceivably yield some results for the COO, but will be far from achieving the full potential benefits. But the implications are actually worse than that. By pursuing a process management implementation in only one part of the organization, despite multiple touch points with other parts of the organization, it becomes difficult to get the processes fully under control. Furthermore, it is difficult to fully enforce process compliance when other parts of the organization are under no such obligation. Finally it also increases the risk that different parts of the organization pursue different implementation plans for process management – and approach which is almost certain to create inefficiencies, as well as create significant problems for larger digitization programs.

The same argument applies to the links between headquarter, regional offices and local agencies. A concerted effort at process management must encompass all of these entities – including 3rd party agencies where the shipping line do not use their own offices.

As already mentioned, process management is an old discipline, although one that is not yet well utilized in the liner shipping industry. But how will this change in the period until 2025?

A few shipping lines have already embarked on ambitious programs to transform themselves into organizations that are driven by process management principles. The experience gained from these companies indicate that the transformation process is indeed both difficult and complex, and implementation takes quite a number of years. By extension this also means that shipping lines which have not yet embarked on this transformation will not be able to quickly reach the level of process maturity exhibited by the first movers.

That process management makes a substantial impact on productivity can be seen when one studies the relation between the number of land-based employees in major shipping lines and the number of containers they move annually. Not all shipping lines publish numbers allowing one to make such a calculation, but for the shipping lines who do, two main conclusions can be drawn based on the numbers for 2015 and 2016.

First of all, there is no correlation between the size of a shipping line and the implied efficiency of its workforce. In other words there is no scale advantage to be seen, and hence the difference in efficiency must be mainly due to differences in how the shipping lines handle their business processes. By logical extension this implies that all shipping lines should be able to improve their efficiency levels to match the best in class. Should the entire liner shipping industry manage to do this it would result in a global reduction of 31.000 people.

Secondly, the best performing shipping line has an efficiency of 19.3 TEU per employee per week. Clearly "employee" here is an average term and covers a very wide variety of job functions across both front office and back end functions. Nonetheless, once we contemplate the implications of further process improvements in conjunction with digitization and automation it is clear that this level of efficiency will be significantly improved. As a hypothetical example, an improvement of just 10% of this level across the entire industry would result in a situation where the liner shipping industry as a whole would start to reduce the total land based workforce by 25%.

A shipping line which has achieved a high degree of maturity in process management will be poised to accelerate their implementation of digitization and automation. A high degree of process maturity implies that it is feasible to shift a range of business processes away from manual handling and into automated handling. This furthermore implies that the significant amounts of jobs which will be made redundant are in the majority linked to business processes which lend themselves to automation. Those would principally be the functions which over the past 15 years have been outsourced to major global service centers.

Functions which have been successfully transferred to global service centers are characterised by on one hand being relatively standard processes, but on the other hand not being sufficiently standardised to automate them yet. This is what will be changing over the coming decade. The shipping lines who are the most mature in the way of managing processes will be the first to shift out of the service centers and into automated applications.

For the less mature shipping lines, their challenge lies in acknowledging the need for process management and to embark on a transformation strategy. If they wait until they see competing shipping lines shifting into automated processes they will be at a significant cost disadvantage for several years. This drive to automation cannot be resolved by spending significant amounts of resources on an IT project. Multiple shipping lines have attempted this, only to realize that their processes were not sufficiently under control to achieve this aim, and instead a solution involving global service centers had to be used.

Action Point: Process Management

Looking towards 2025 it is clear that a number of shipping lines have already progressed along a trajectory towards placing process management at the centre of how they manage their business. They will continue along this trajectory as the data clearly indicate a significant efficiency gain from doing so.

The action plan in relation to process management therefore depends on where the individual company is on this trajectory. For companies being relatively mature, the next step is the shift into automation for an increasing number of processes.

For companies which are either at an early stage on this trajectory, or who have not yet begun the transformation, it is strategically vital to do so. This does not mean they all have to embrace process management in exactly the same fashion. Nor does it imply they need identical processes – quite the contrary, as processes need to be developed to be efficient within the specific context of a specific company. But failure to embark on this transformation is exceedingly likely to place the company in a position where they are no longer a viable major competitor by 2025.

Key questions for exploration for an individual company:

What is your level of maturity in terms process management?

How do I ensure my processes are well defined, and well executed, prior to launching any IT projects to automate them?

How efficient am I in my usage of personnel relative to my competitor and the industry?

In which sequence do I plan to automate my processes?

What is my long term plan for transitioning standard processes away from service centers and into automated applications?

The Impact of Transparency

The shipping industry if often labelled as an "invisible industry". Usually this is because the average person, not involved with the industry, rarely considers how his goods were moved to reach the shelves in the supermarket. This has for many years served the industry well, as that has also implied that business practices could take place away from sometimes critical eyes. Furthermore, the commercial relationships in liner shipping are often more akin to horse-trading practices than to 21st century scientific sourcing and pricing principles. All of this is under rapid change – partly by developments spurred on by the shipping lines themselves, and partly by outside forces.

The increased transparency will impact a number of very different parameters, and in the following we will take a look at the impact it will have on pricing, the environment and service failures.

Pricing transparency

The impact on pricing is already being felt by an industry still trying to come to grips with new and more transparent price indices. Whereas several indices preceded it, the launch of the Shanghai Container Freight Index (SCFI) by the Shanghai Shipping Exchange in 2010 is the best example of the impact transparency is having. Prior to this, the rate levels in the spot market were at the same time both opaque and transparent.

They were opaque because there was no place to go to for market participants to get an easy, and frequently updated, overview of the spot rate development in the market. At the same time they were transparent to the participants in the market. A shipper would quite simply call a range of shipping lines and ask for price quotes in order to gauge the level of the market. Similarly shipping lines would use the feedback from customers to gauge the strength of the proposed rate levels – and in some cases might even call competitors using a false name to gauge their rate levels. Whilst this provided market participants with tactical information, it did not provide a common reference for both parties in the negotiation to agree upon.

As mentioned, a number of indices got launched, but until now the SCFI have likely had the largest impact on the broader understanding of rate developments in the market. This is unlikely to continue until 2025, but in order to understand the changes it is bringing, and why other indices will take over, let us take a look at the impact of the SCFI.

Originally the SCFI was designed as an index to support the launch of freight rate derivatives. The derivatives were financial instruments intended to be used for risk management purposes by shippers, shipping lines and financial parties. Most major shipping lines regarded the freight rate derivatives as a strategic threat, and in order to eliminate that threat, one of the tools employed was an attempt at delegitimizing the SCFI as not being credible.

The SCFI is not a perfect index as it is based only on a sample of data, and hence any shipper or shipping line can perfectly well claim that their specific rate does not match the SCFI. It can even be that the majority of cargo is shipped at a rate level different from that indicated by the SCFI. The shipping lines, correctly, made this assertion and used it as an argument as to why the SCFI should not play a role in freight rate negotiations.

However, the SCFI was also an index which quickly became very visible in the industry. Furthermore it was easy to understand as it was stating rate levels in actual USD per TEU rather than an abstract index figure. For a vast range of shippers this was the first time they were able to get a weekly standardized overview of spot rates on a range of key trade corridors.

Additionally, the simplicity and visibility of the index lend itself well to the shipping press. With new spot rates being published at the end of each week, it provided a good fix point to give a journalistic take on whether the week had seen a weakening of the market or whether the shipping lines had been successful with the latest round of rate increases.

Hereafter it became a self-fulfilling prophecy. Even though the index rates did not necessarily reflect the actual spot rates to be paid, it was now being used by the shippers in their negotiations with the shipping lines. As the market was heading into overcapacity, the pricing power shifted towards the shippers, and as they were guided by the SCFI, consequently the underlying rates would increasingly also be impacted by the SCFI. At a number of shipping conferences in 2015-16 this gave rise to a more philosophical debate as to whether the very existence of the SCFI, and similar indices, were partly to blame for the rapid escalation in rate volatility and the outright collapse of freight rates in some trades, or whether the SCFI was simply a tool which shed a light on those unfavourable developments.

Herein we see a very clear example of what happens when transparency partially intrudes on a part of the industry which is not used to such transparency. In the absence of highly visible indices, freight rates were negotiated directly between a shipper and a shipping line. Both parties likely had a good feel for the market levels, and hence were satisfied. But as rate levels are made visible it results in several new dynamics.

First of all it reduces the ability for the shipping line to price individually to each shipper, and it particularly reduces the shipping line's ability to change rate levels by amounts that differ from the changes reflected in the rate index.

For the shipper this also had unintended consequences. In many companies the procurement of freight is typically handled by a supply chain manager. As the core business of the shipper is not supply chain management but the production or sales of various trade goods, the supply chain manager often operated outside of the spotlight of the main business. With the high degree of visibility awarded by the shipping press, this meant that senior managers within the shippers became aware of the freight rate developments. A supply chain manager would therefore increasingly be asked the following question by his CEO: "I saw the freight rates declined 10% this week – when will I see that on your budget?".

For supply chain managers who focused on generating a stable, predictable and efficient supply chain they were often signed up for contracts with durations of up to 12 months, and as such not subject to the swings of the spot market. Many would therefore provide pushback on the CEO and explain this to him. However, as the volatility continued to increase in the spot markets, the contract rates were increasingly seen as significantly out of touch with the spot market, eventually pushing the supply chain managers to use the spot index as an argument to renegotiate contract rates.

It is also clear that the shipping lines in general have not been prepared to handle this increased level of transparency in terms of their pricing processes. The pricing processes in themselves is a topic for scrutiny in later section pertaining to yield management, but essentially they were to a significant degree based on the intransparency of the markets. It would therefore be correct to conclude that the advent of transparent rate indices have indeed had a direct impact on the price formation. What cannot be concluded, however, is the magnitude of the impact. As previously mentioned the market participants already had some indication of pricing levels in the market – the rate index only added two components.

One component was related to efficiency. Rather than spending time to obtain quotes from multiple shipping lines to gauge the markets, shippers could save time and simply refer to the spot rate index. This in all likelihood means that they would more often than before check the market rates prior to negotiating with a shipping line.

The other component was related to misrepresentation of the rate levels. The spot index is related to a relatively narrow range of shipper needs and corridors. Hence for substantial amounts of cargo the actual market rate would differ, and at times differ markedly. But in the absence of other information, this component would also have had an impact on the rate formation.

The past 5 years have seen an increase in the amount of rate indices available. Some, like the SCFI, are publicly available, others are available only against a subscription fee. They have different methodologies for sourcing their data with some getting the data from shipping lines, some from freight forwarders and NVOCCs and some directly from the shippers. Some indices have been created to provide more clarity on spot rates, whereas other are specifically targeted at helping to create transparency on contract rates solely for very large shippers with large contractual commitments. Some of these indices clearly have a stronger methodology and depth in their datasets than others. But the mere fact that the number of providers of freight indices is growing, and that the geographical spread of the coverage of these indices is growing, shows a significant demand on the part of the shippers for this type of transparency.

As spot rates are beginning to be shown online, the transparency into such rates will only continue to increase. This raises a few important issues for both shippers and carriers.

As a shipper it becomes increasingly important to understand exactly what a specific price index measures, and in turn whether this is relevant for the cargo in scope. A spot index is for example a poor tool to use for benchmarking pricing on 12-month contracts, and similarly rate levels measured for certain specific commodity types such as for example wastepaper or scrap metal might be poor indicators for the shipment of garments or furniture.

As a shipping line, there are two fundamental questions which must be addressed. Whilst a shipping line might not want to see additional transparency, the development over the past 5 years will continue to accelerate and by 2025 rate indices will be readily available for vast range of trades and cargo types.

The first question a carrier need to examine is how to devise a pricing strategy which works in a transparent environment. Rather than seeing the rate indices as a disruptive force, it becomes necessary to accept them as an integral part of the market dynamics.

If the assessment is that the indices are detrimental to the pricing strategy, the only viable path forward is to devise a pricing strategy for which the indices are not detrimental. Part of the potential solution to this was mentioned previously in the section discussing the advent of new enforceable contract types. Currently the spot rate indices can be perceived as disruptive, as shippers can easily renege on already agreed-on bookings when they see the spot indices change rapidly. Another part of the solution lies in the active use of yield management tools.

The second question a shipping line needs to examine is to which degree they should assist in the development of transparent rate indices.

The current indices clearly have a range of flaws, but as already mentioned, they are heavily used by the shippers simply because they are easily available. Some of the more fundamental flaws include the use of a limited number of price points with which to determine the rate level, lack of clarity in terms of which surcharges or land-side charges are included in the levels, lack of clarity in terms of which shipping lines are included as they do not all have the exact same pricing levels and in some cases the inclusion of freight rate levels which are part of a contract but against which no cargo is actually being booked.

All of these are arguments supporting shipping lines in their notion that indices can be detrimental to the dynamics in the market. But ignoring them, or assuming that they will disappear over time will not solve the problem for the shipping lines. Instead they have a very fundamental choice to make. They can either leave the indices alone, thereby ensuring the continued development of rate indices will take place without influence from the shipping lines. Or they can actively engage in the development of rate indices.

In this context it should be noted that engaging actively in the development of better rate indices is not a simple matter. First and foremost this has to be done within the confines of competitive legislation which in some geographies place strict limits on how shipping lines can engage in such activities. Secondly it would have to be done in a fashion whereby their involvement is genuinely perceived as adding value and accuracy to the index – not seen as an attempt to manipulate the perception of freight rates. A good example of what not to do was illustrated by the TSA (Transpacific Stabilization Agreement) which is a group of carriers on the Transpacific trade. Apparently dismayed by the SCFI spot rate index, they launched an index in 2011 to cover rate developments on the Transpacific trade. In the very definition of the index it was stated that the purpose of the index was to create rate stability – as opposed to the other indices in the market at the time which all had it as their mission to provide information showing the rate developments. Any attempt at using an index to influence market behaviour, and aiming at creating market stability is indeed an attempt to influence market behaviour, is likely to fail over time – simply because the shippers need to perceive the data as being impartial.

Therefore the combination of these two key question boils down to whether the carriers in 2025 want to be part of providing rate transparency which is as accurate as possible, or whether they want to operate in a market where their customers are partly relying on freight rate information which is purely under the control of 3rd parties.

Environmental transparency

Transparency on the environmental performance is a topic where the shipping lines began being active as far back as in 2002 where the foundation was laid for what is currently known as the Clean Cargo Work Group (CCWG). This group was established out of a desire from shippers to obtain more insights into the environmental performance of the shipping lines.

The early work provided by the CCWG was a good case study of what it takes to achieve transparency even in a straight-forward situation when all parties agree this is what needs to happen. In order to create true transparency, it was necessary to develop measurement standards for a variety of issues such as e.g. CO_2 emissions. Without standards every shipping line would measure their environmental performance differently. The result would be that everyone could claim to be transparent in showing their performance, but in reality there would be no transparency at all, as it would be impossible to compare performance in a meaningful way.

Over the course of several years, measurement standards were agreed upon, leading to a situation allowing for a significant improvement in transparency on some environmental parameters. The ability of the shipping lines and the shippers to collaborate in setting such standards indicate a capability which might be well applied going forward.

However, it is equally clear that the complexities inherent in a supply chain which encompasses much more than simply moving a large container vessel from point A to point B, leads to the standards not always capturing the full and accurate picture. This is where both shippers and shipping lines have varying perceptions. For some it is perfectly fine to provide transparency using a methodology which is mostly, but not completely, correct. For others this is not an acceptable level of accuracy.

The consequence is that despite, for example, the CO2 emissions calculation having been in place for many years, it is not provided automatically by all shipping lines – in turn reducing the level of transparency which could have been obtained.

As the environmental focus is increasingly getting political attention this means that to the extend the shipping industry cannot develop and implement effective, and transparent, standards, ultimately there will be legislation doing this instead.

The transparency of environmental performance in the supply chain is completely invisible to the end consumer. Even those consumers who place a high focus on environmental performance will not have the slightest opportunity to know how a particular product came to be delivered to the local supermarket, let alone know which shipping line moved it across the ocean. Hence, unlike consumer goods companies, the shipping lines are under no direct customer pressure to provide additional transparency.

Some shippers have in recent years begun to scrutinize all their suppliers, including shipping lines, in terms of their environmental performance, but these are clearly in the minority.

Looking ahead towards 2025 it remains unrealistic to believe that the end consumer will have any preference for particular shipping companies, as shipping is only a minor part of the environmental footprint of a given product.

However, it is exceedingly likely that we will see more cargo owners, particularly in Europe and the US, demand increased levels of transparency in terms of environmental performance. For the shipping lines this is clearly an opportunity as, all else being equal, the environmental footprint of moving cargo in containers across the ocean is much smaller than moving the same amounts of goods over land or by air.

The key problem the shipping lines will be facing comes from increased legislative pressure. Container shipping is, by far, the most environmentally friendly way to transport large amounts of cargo over extended distances. However, the sheer amount of cargo moved globally also means that the total amount of emissions stemming from the shipping lines is a sizeable proportion of the overall global emissions. The increased focus on the environment in general is also making shipping's overall emissions visible and transparent.

The increased level of transparency results in political pressure to reduce emissions, and in turn results in legislation to improve performances. In recent years, this has given rise to a variety of regulations such as the low-Sulphur regulation was initially implemented in North Europe and USA, and is currently being phased-in in certain parts of the China and from 2020 to be extended globally.

This is not to imply that the regulation is wrong, nor to imply that it is a direct consequence of the transparency. However it is to indicate that as environmental performance continues to grow in importance, the shipping lines will increasingly find themselves in situations where they need to account for their own performance. And in order to do this in a meaningful way they need to continue to develop standards for an increasing array of environmental parameters in order to live up to the requirements for transparency.

The choice is not whether or not to increase the level of environmental transparency. The choice is to which degree the shipping lines want to actively participate in the developments of the standards. And herein lies an aspect which has not yet come to the forefront.

As is covered in the chapter pertaining to automation, the vessels are being outfitted with a multitude of sensors measuring an expanding array of performance parameters. These sensors are additionally designed to transmit their data online from any location globally, and are becoming an integrated part of the Internet of Things. The driving force is a desire to increase the efficiency of the vessel through Big Data analysis.

But a side effect of this escalation in available data is that shipping lines over the coming years will be able to design data applications to measure the environmental performance on a wide range of parameters as well. In order to do this, standards will have to be developed.

Presently shipping lines are not at the same state of development in terms of installing such online sensors. Some are rapidly upgrading their fleet with the new technology, others have not yet begun. At the time of launching the Clean Cargo Work Group, the participating shipping lines were, technically speaking, all adequately equipped to contribute to the development of the standards. For shipping lines which have not yet begun to plan for significant implementation of on-board sensors and associated Big Data analytics for operational purposes, they need to ask themselves whether they this time around are adequately equipped to participate in the development of environmental standards for 2025. And if the answer to that question is no, whether they would feel comfortable leaving that development to the shipping lines who have progressed the furthest, as that will otherwise de facto become the reality.

Service failures and supply chain visibility

As mentioned in the section about exception management, this is an industry with a multitude of service failures. Some are preventable and others are simply issues of force majeure.

The increasing levels of transparency will have the consequence that shippers will become aware of service failures at an increasing speed, and ultimately they will know about a service failure at the same time as the shipping lines.

Let us break this down into a range of different service failures and examine how the transparency will change the approach of shippers and carriers.

At first there is the simple matter of a vessel arriving late into port. This is a very common occurrence. Despite being the best year since 2011, measurements from SeaIntel Maritime Analysis shows that 18% of all deep-sea container vessels arrived more the 1 day late in 2016.

In the past, shippers would only discover this problem either when the shipping line told them, or when it became apparent to them that the vessel was physically not present in the port.

Following the initial wave of eCommerce tools from the shipping lines in the early 2000's one of the first applications to become widespread across the shipping lines' websites, was the ability for shippers to track the location of their container. This did improve visibility to some degree for shippers, although the accuracy of the tracking applications varied significantly across carriers, and to some degree it still does. It relies upon the shipping line's backend systems being able to match the location of the actual container with the location of the vessel. This would typically include an operational systems keeping track of the actual sailing schedule of the vessel, an equipment systems matching containers to their locations whether on a vessel, in a port or in a depot as well as a match against a booking database wherein, ideally, information is stored pertaining to the delivery time which was stated on the booking confirmation.

Whilst it in theory should be a simple matter to inter-link these systems, the actual IT infrastructure for many shipping lines makes this a process which can be both severely time delayed as well as error prone. The tracking application has therefore drastically improved visibility, but not always made it perfect.

Increasingly developments are being undertaken to take visibility to a much more accurate level, including visibility into expected delays.

One development is related to the AIS transponders all vessels are equipped with. This makes the location of each individual vessel available to everyone, and not just to the shipping lines. This allows a shipper to track the progress of the vessel independently of the information received from the shipping lines. Furthermore this allows the shipper to notice a delay far in advance of the vessel getting to the destination port. Seemingly he can use this to forecast a service failure – or possibly a 3rd party service company can provide such a service to shippers, proactively forecasting service failures.

This is the point where the transparency has the potential of creating work for both shippers and shipping lines which is not value-adding.

Take the example of a vessel going from Shanghai to Rotterdam. It is scheduled to call Singapore en route, but gets 2 days delayed by a typhoon. A shipper who monitors the progress of the vessel will notice the vessel is 2 days delayed on arrival in Singapore. The shipper might at this point contact the shipping line and ask what they intend to do about the delay. Upon conferring with the operations department, the shipping line might subsequently inform the shipper, that they plan to speed up the vessel, and will be arriving on time in Rotterdam.

At first glance this has created a satisfied shipper who was reassured that his cargo would be on time, and a customer service representative who could assuage the concerns of the shipper.

But on second glance, both parties have wasted time and effort. Shipping lines should strive to extract data streams from the operational systems, including the capturing of any decisions to change speed or other parameters, and use such data to enhance the information presented as part of the tracking applications. A shipper contacts the shipping line if he is concerned that there might be a non-conformance. The shipping line needs to develop its information based on the assumption that the shipper has access to the same level of present and historical operational performance as the shipping line itself. What the shipper does not have any transparency into, are the decisions the shipping line has made pertaining to the operational performance going forward.

Therefore, in the absence of other information, the shipper will likely assume that the sudden appearance of a non-conformance might persist and ultimately impact his cargo as well.

For the shipping line the question therefore becomes one of providing automated information pertaining to anticipated service failures. The key word here is "anticipated", as the service failures can be anticipated either by the shipping line or the shipper. When the shipping line anticipates a service failure, this becomes an exception and the approach to exception handling was considered in the earlier chapter on this topic. However, the increased levels of transparency means that shippers will begin to anticipate service failures as well – even when no such failures are expected by the shipping line. The shipping lines therefore need to contemplate not only how to deal with the genuine exceptions, but also how to proactively provide information dispelling unfounded concerns over potential service failures.

Another type of service failure would be cargo damage. This is of particular concern for reefer shipments where the failure to adhere to specific temperature or atmosphere settings can result in the loss of the entire shipment of goods. Until recently there was no transparency into these service failures until the point where the cargo was received by the customer. If, at that point, it was determined that there was a service failure, the datalog for the specific shipment would have to be manually retrieved from the container in question.

This is changing with some shipping lines beginning to feature online data loggers on the reefer containers which are accessible through an internet connection via the vessel's satellite uplink while at sea, and via mobile network connection while on land. Such devices create real-time transparency into the condition of the cargo. Not only does this allow the cargo receiver to get a pre-warning if the cargo for some reason gets spoilt en route, thus allowing him to arrange for alternate options. But it also allows the monitoring of the loading conditions, enabling the ability to determine whether damaged reefer cargo was damaged due to the shipment or due to the conditions at the loading itself.

This is an element of transparency which not only addresses the aspect of service failure, but also increases the level of supply chain visibility to a level not previously attainable. It allows cargo owners to document the full end-to-end storage conditions of cargo susceptible to for example temperature swings.

But online loggers will not remain the realm solely of reefer containers. The advantage of reefers is the fact that they are powered and thus makes it logistically simple to equip them with such loggers. The slightly more complex aspect of the operation is to equip the vessel with a mobile network allowing to bridge the connection between the mobile logging device and the vessel's satellite uplink.

The next step, which has already been trialled by several shipping lines, is to equip dry containers with online GPS equipped tracking devices as well. If vessels are already becoming equipped with mobile networks in order to provide an uplink for the reefer containers, the business case for the dry containers becomes more favourable.

In terms of addressing cargo damage, there is much less of a business value as opposed to the reefer cargo. However, by having accelerometers being a part of the data logger, it is possible to measure whether a particular shipment has been exposed to excessive forces by for example being dropped.

The value of transparency by equipping dry containers with tracking devices is to be found in the supply chain visibility this provides. Providing end-to-end visibility is presently difficult to achieve. The shipping line may well be able to combine the vessel's AIS position and the vessel's load plan to inform of the position while on the vessel. However, this does not provide visibility into the location on the land side. At best a shipper might know a container has been picked up or dropped off at a specific location, but apart from this, visibility is limited. For short inland journeys this is a limited issue, where for long multi-day inland journeys it becomes a different matter.

Additionally, equipping the dry containers with online tracking devices provides two additional opportunities for shipping lines.

One opportunity is primarily of relevance if the data quality in the shipping line's equipment systems is not high, or the data does not flow instantly between varying systems creating problems with time delayed data streams. In this case, the introduction of live trackers on all containers can create a perfect, updated, overview of the equipment situation at any point in time, including not only cargo en route to a customer, but also the flow of empty containers as well as the real-time availability of containers in depots.

This aspect also leads to the second opportunity – and an opportunity a number of companies have been piloting for a while. Having real-time data pertaining to the equipment movements allows for optimization of the empty equipment flows. It allows for matching the need for one customer to redeliver an empty container to a depot, with the need for another customer to pick up an empty container. If they are located advantageously related to each other versus in relation to the depot, that could save substantial costs on the trucking side. Conversely, allowing trucking companies access to these data flows would allow for a better usage of the trucks by reducing the distance driven with no containers on the trailer.

Over the next decade towards 2025, it appears certain that reefer containers will become equipped with live trackers as a standard, as the business value to the customers is significant.

As for the tracking of the dry containers, it seems likely that this will also happen, although the business case for this is not as obvious at the moment as for the reefer containers. This is not only related to costs of the trackers themselves, but also related to the fact that if the shipping lines manage to successfully upgrade their data quality and IT infrastructure, and combine this with data feeds from the GPS trackers on the trucks they use on the land side, almost the same level of transparency can be accomplished for the dry containers as with a tracker.

For the shippers, achieving real-time end-to-end supply chain visibility, with pro-active notifications when service failures are expected is a clear improvement in the value provided by the shipping lines. One aspect they should consider, however, are the ramifications of such transparency on their own operations.

Just as the AIS transponders on vessels have led to a situation where anyone can track the whereabouts of a vessel – unless the transponder is turned off, or is deliberately set to emit false information – having real-time tracking devices on all containers might well lead to a situation where the same effect can be accomplished at the container level. It is less easy to accomplish than for the AIS transponders, but in essence all containers would be identifying themselves on the mobile communication networks.

If it is possible to "tag" a container, it becomes possible to map out the full journey of the container. Once that is accomplished, the start and end points can be matched with a specific address, which in turn can be cross-referenced with business information directories listing not only known companies' locations, but also their main distribution centers. This would ultimately allow anyone with access to the data to map out the major parts of the supply chains for all shippers globally, and by extension map out where and when cargo flows to and from specific vendors changes.

Hence an aspect of transparency which is developed to deal with improving supply chain visibility and allow for better contingency planning in cases of service failures, will also give rise to significant opportunities for improved equipment management as well as bring about the potential for 3rd parties to gain significant market intelligence on the supply chains of all shippers globally.

Action Point: Transparency

Looking towards 2025, the liner shipping industry will shift from being an "invisible" industry, and the pricing dynamics will similarly reach a much different level of transparency than has historically been the case.

Furthermore, the level of supply chain visibility will increase dramatically as a result of the use of live tracking technologies in combination with analytics allowing the pro-active identification of service failures.

The transparency will increasingly extend to environmental performance where sensors intended to improve operational efficiency on the vessels can be leveraged to provide real-time measurements of emissions.

A very important lesson to take away from the increase in transparency is the fact that informational advantages in negotiations will be drastically eroded. Hence any stakeholders in the industry who use informational advantage as a key part of their commercial success will need to change this part of their business model.

Key questions:

How do you plan to change your pricing strategy to adopt to a market of high transparency?

What are your plans to assist in developing more accurate price indices?

As a shipper, how do you know whether a given index accurately depicts rates that are relevant for you?

How do you plan to provide information pertaining to anticipated service failures?

How do you plan to provide end-to-end supply chain visibility for both dry and reefer containers?

How are you planning to use on board sensors to develop transparent measurement of environmental performance?

How do you plan to engage in developing the standards for environmental transparency?

As a shipper, how do you plan to use the increased amounts of data the live supply chain visibility will result in?

To which degree do we rely on having more information than our negotiation partner, and how will we change our behaviour as that advantage is eroded?

The advent of Yield Management

Yield management in this context is a broad topic associated with the combination of pricing, uptake management, capacity management and cost transparency. Every shipping line needs to get a combined system in place to have these issues handled. Some shipping lines have already been using elements of yield management for several years, whereas some are in the process of developing their first comprehensive systems for this.

At the outset it all sounds deceptively simple. It is all about accepting the right cargo at the right price. Where it stops being simple is when we begin to explore what "the right cargo" is, and what "the right price is".

Cost transparency

Let us start at the level of costs. A typical problem for shipping lines is that many cost elements are often only known with a great degree of delay. This is caused by a multitude of factors. Some costs are variable and only known with precision once the service has been received. In these cases, an assessment of cost at the time of determining the appropriate freight rate is based partially on assumptions. Other costs are fixed irrespective of the number of containers which are booked, and hence a unit cost assessment must necessarily include assumptions pertaining to the anticipated booking volumes. The last problem relating to costs is the relatively poor administrative IT infrastructure in many shipping lines. It is not uncommon that it can take months for a variety of cost elements to be properly updated within the internal systems, in turn making it even more difficult to make accurate assessments of costs at the time of pricing.

There are two paths through which the knowledge of cost will become drastically improved going forward. One relates to the administrative challenges. That this is a problem today is a reflection of the lack of proper process management in the industry, as depicted in the earlier chapter, in combination with administrative IT systems which are not designed to support a holistic approach to yield management. The path to improvement lies in a complete overhaul of the processes within the liner shipping companies, and in conjunction with this, a re-think of the administrative systems. These systems should be designed from the perspective that their primary function is not only financial reporting, but equally that they need to be seen as integral parts of real-time commercial systems.

The other important path towards getting better cost transparency is improved forecasting. This is specifically targeted at improving the understanding of unit costs in the face of high fixed costs. This is more complex than initially meets the eye, when the complex scope of the liner shipping network is taken into account.

In a simple case, the anticipated unit cost for a shipment from Shanghai to Rotterdam depends partly on the anticipated vessel utilization. The more accurately I can forecast the amount of bookings from Shanghai, the more accurately I can forecast my unit costs. This applies equally in the tactical sense where I contemplate the unit costs for this week's sailing, as well as in the strategic sense where I contemplate my average unit costs over the coming quarter.

In reality this becomes much more complex, as the aforementioned sailing from Shanghai to Rotterdam will stop in half a dozen ports along the way to take additional cargo on board. Additionally, parts of the cargo is destined for Africa and will be transhipped to a feeder service along the way.

The challenge then becomes how to improve forecasting in order to improve the understanding of costs. There are two primary tools with which to do this. The reason for this is that there are two conceptually different sources of uncertainty. One is related to the ability to forecast future bookings, the other is related to whether cargo, which has already been booked or contractually committed, will even turn up.

One of the tools has already been contemplated – that is the introduction of enforceable contracts. Both for short-term spot cargo as well as for longer term contractual relations. As already seen, the developments over the coming decade will result in an environment of much higher enforceability of contracts. This in itself will result in a higher degree of forecasting accuracy, whereby the ability to forecast unit costs will be improved on this parameter.

The other tool pertains to the ability to forecast future bookings as well future developments in other relevant cost parameters. When delving into this topic one must distinguish between the forecasting of endogenous and exogenous parameters. Exogenous parameters are aspects which are independent of the actions taken by the shipping line, whereas endogenous parameters are aspects upon which the shipping line has an element of influence. The forecasting of oil prices is an exogenous parameter, as no shipping line has the ability to materially impact the development of oil prices. On the other hand, the forecasting of the exact number of bookings to be taken in a specific location is an endogenous parameter as this will depend partially on for example the pricing offered by the shipping line itself, or the change of dedicated sales efforts towards particular clients.

How the shipping lines are going to improve these two aspects of forecasting in the future will be separated into two subsections below. The first will contemplate the exogenous parameters. The second will contemplate the endogenous parameters and will revolve about the merging of pricing, booking uptake and capacity management.

Exogenous forecasting

Exogenous parameters are typically macroeconomic developments of relevance to the shipping line. At the highest levels it will be forecasts of trade growth, fuel prices, currency exchange rates etc. At a slightly more granular level it will be the forecast of cargo flows for specific commodity types, specific customer types or even individual large shippers.

For the macroeconomic parameters, a shipping line needs to consider whether they have, or aspire to have, the macroeconomic skills to provide the best possible forecasts. Will the company be able to produce forecasts at a level of sophistication matching the skill level available from external companies who specialize in such forecasts? A realistic assessment would be that almost no shipping lines would be able to provide the environment wherein their forecasting abilities on the macro parameters could match specialized external providers.

Subsidiary to this question, a shipping line needs to contemplate whether an internal forecast of exogenous parameters is a wise decision. In any organization there is always the risk of bias, and if the forecast of exogenous parameters suddenly does not match the aspiration in a new strategy plan, the temptation, whether conscious or subconscious, is high to modify the forecasts slightly.

Going forward we will not be seeing shipping lines aspire to produce their own forecasts of exogenous parameters. This will be – and already is in many companies – the realm of external experts.

However, what the shipping lines need to develop is the ability to apply the exogenous macroeconomic forecasts within their own organizations. This requires an approach where the forecasts are "translated" into elements of relevance for the endogenous parameters – and where it is made clear in the organization, that the exogenous parameters cannot be overruled to serve a need to show a slightly more positive – or negative – outlook. If any forecasts have to be changed, it must be the endogenous parameters.

At the more granular level, exogenous parameters would be the forecast of localized trade flows as well as the flow of specific commodities of customer groupings. In these cases it can be relevant for a shipping line to contemplate whether they would want to develop this expertise internally or rely on external sourcing.

Presently, a key the problem related to this forecasting is the lack of transparency in many markets. For many trade lanes, no solid statistical databases exist pertaining to the exact amount of containers being shipped, let alone broken down at a commodity or customer level. A few countries do provide such statistics, with the USA as a primary example, but these are currently the exceptions. Without a solid baseline of current and historical data, forecasting accuracy will suffer. 3rd party databases providing some of these elements exist, but they too have to rely on modelling efforts where primary data sources simply do not exist. In the short to medium term this means the especially large shipping lines may arrive at the conclusion that for markets without solid primary data, their own strong presence in the market gives them the ability to assess and model the market dynamics with a larger accuracy and granularity than external parties. Smaller shipping lines do not realistically have this option.

However, when the developments out to 2025 are considered, this view will have to change as well. As we have already seen, transparency is rapidly increasing and in all likelihood this will happen to the data pertaining to container trade flows as well. The few places that currently provide accurate granular data do this by making data from customs authorities available. It could be considered that an increased number of authorities would begin to make such data available. However, given the slow development of such organizations, and the requirements placed upon them from national governments, it does not appear likely that this path would lead to transparency of all major trade flows at a granular level by 2025.

The primary data pertaining to the actual trade flows are also held by a number of different stakeholders, all of whom might be in a position to leverage this into a transparent database of cargo flows.

Container terminals have detailed data showing the load/unload of individual containers by container number, as well as whether the container is full or empty. Simply matching these data would be sufficient to create a detailed mapping of cargo flows, albeit not at a commodity and customer level.

Major local and global eCommerce portals have a flow of data which would allow for a very accurate mapping, not only at the container level, but also at the commodity and customer level – especially if data from multiple portals were leveraged into one analytical system.

An independent entity could conceivably collect data streams from a vast range of freight forwarders and major cargo owners, and from this create an overview of major trade flows at the commodity level.

As mentioned previously, when all containers become outfitted with GPS tracking devices, this opens the opportunity for 3rd parties to accurately map trade flows, and by leveraging informational databases pertaining to major cargo owners also break this down by shipper.

Of course there is an additional source of data available – the shipping lines themselves. By combining all of their data it would of course be possible to create the most accurate database of them all. To some degree this already exists through the entity called Container Trade Statistics. However this has a couple of important limitations. First of all only a limited number of shipping lines provide data. Secondly, and more importantly, especially the European competition law has placed significant restrictions on the provision of such data by the shipping lines. This is a historic consequence of the old conference systems which was abolished in Europe in 2008. This has led to a high degree of suspicion from authorities that shipping lines will attempt to use accurate market data to collude. Consequently the timeliness and granularity of the data which can be provided is somewhat restricted.

Hence when we look forward to 2025 it is clear, that multiple fundamentally different avenues exist for creating, and providing, databases, which provide much more transparent insights into the overall container trade flows.

The key question for the shipping lines is therefore how they would prefer to see this transparency be developed. As we saw in the case of freight rate indices, a lack of transparency into market data will simply lead to the launch of databases which may be imperfect, but better than the prevailing status. Thus, the shipping lines can choose to enter into collaborative work through entities controlled by themselves to create the transparency, or they can choose to engage with third parties to facilitate the development. Abstaining from participating in the development will lead to third parties providing the transparency through other sources, not necessarily fully matching the shipping lines' view.

But all of this was simply the data foundation for understanding the current and historical markets – a foundation necessary to improve the exogenous forecasts.

Given the transparency into current container flows, this can be combined with the macro economic forecasts to provide more detailed insights. It can be the forecasts at a commodity level – i.e. what is the expected flow of textiles or furniture on a given trade lane over the next quarter. Or it can be the forecast for an industry such as what is the anticipated growth rate for the retail sector in a specific country over the next quarter, and how does that translate into changes in container flows.

For this type of forecasting, major shipping lines are in a position to likely be the best at developing accurate forecasts, as they have the ability to combine the factual historical and present data with both quantifiable insights based on their own customers' ordering patterns as well as more unstructured data pertaining to information provided to the sales people through conversations with clients. Of particular importance is the ability to obtain information pertaining to changes in inventory levels as well as shifts in sourcing patterns or plans to expand operations in certain areas.

Moving towards 2025, this is where shipping lines with a detailed and structured approach towards Big Data will have an advantage. One of the key value points of Big Data is the ability to integrate highly diverse data streams, which means leveraging the, future, high degree of visibility into existing cargo flows, with less quantifiable data pertaining to the customers' changing trade and behaviour patterns.

Overall this will lead to a situation where shipping lines will be able to reduce the uncertainty on exogenous variables, but clearly will still be subject to the forecasting uncertainties always inherent in such models.

Pricing, Booking uptake and Capacity Management

Whereas the forecast of exogenous parameters are critical when performing strategic planning, the forecasting of endogenous parameters are substantially more important when it comes to immediate commercial yield management considerations. By 2025, we will have reached a point where only shipping lines who practice a structured approach to yield management will be profitable.

The baseline for any shipping line is to ensure a complete merger between the disciplines of pricing, booking uptake and capacity management. This is the core of yield management, and is an approach which has been implemented with substantial success over the past decades in industries such as hotels and airlines. Both of these are industries which – like the shipping industry – are selling a completely perishable commodity. If a hotel room is not booked on a given night, the potential revenue is lost forever. The same applies to an empty airline seat. For the shipping lines, this is more nuanced. A vessel which departs Shanghai for Europe with unfilled slots have not entirely lost the revenue. As it calls additional ports before leaving Asia, the shipping line has multiple different options for selling a slot which was initially not filled. But ultimately the problem remains the same – an empty slot is essentially a product which is being produced and paid for, but does not provide any revenue.

The potential value of this approach is significant, and it is estimated that companies which have successfully embarked on structured yield management programs see a yield increase of 2-5% compared to the industry average over a period of 3-5 years. With the drive towards commoditization in the industry, this is a difference which no major shipping line can leave behind.

For many shipping lines, structured yield management programs are not the standard. Instead pricing, capacity management and booking uptake tend to be relatively poorly integrated. Many different models for each of these disciplines are currently in operation within the shipping industry, with some clearly being more structured than others. Outlining all of these would fill an entire book in itself. A few illustrative examples of the practices being as follows: Pricing to fill a certain number of slots in a particular location, having a sales target for sales people in a specific location with bonuses attached for exceeding volume targets and having a rigid allocation of slots on a vessel designated to particular ports.

It is clear that all of these have their merits, especially in terms of simplicity – and furthermore that they were well suited for the rapid growth phase of the industry. But they will no longer be suitable for the industry going forward.

Pricing to fill a certain number of slots in a particular location has the merit of being very simply to implement and manage. In a market with high demand growth this will be generally successful as any build-up of overcapacity will be quickly eliminated. However, in a market with low demand growth this becomes a substantial problem. This is because the liner shipping industry is, in the short term, essentially a zero-sum game. In for example the hotel industry, the price of a room can be lowered, in turn stimulating more demand.

In the liner shipping industry this is not the case. Lowering the freight rate in a given week will not result in any customers wanting to ship additional containers. Their demand for container shipment is governed by the sale of their goods, and as the freight cost is only a very small portion of their overall costs, changing the freight rate will not change the ultimate demand. Exceptions to this exist, with low value cargo such as wastepaper or scrap metal where a high price might dampen demand. Furthermore, pricing changes might shift parts of the demand from one week to another. But the core dynamic is a zero-sum game.

Hence a strategy whereby pricing is used as a tool to fill the vessel becomes counter-productive in a low-growth environment. And if there is sustained overcapacity the consequences can be severe, as is evidently clear on some of the major deep-sea trades. Furthermore, as it is a zero-sum game, it only requires a few carriers to pursue this pricing strategy to force the rates in the entire market to collapse.

When a shipping line operates a vessel calling multiple ports, it is practical to allocate specific volume targets to specific ports. This allows the shipping line to set sales targets for the individual agencies and aim for a certain mix of cargo and customers. The problem arises when bookings do not proceed according to plan. This necessitates a shift in not only cargo allocation, but also in sales effort and without a combination of solid processes and real-time analytics on booking developments, it is not possible to optimize the use of the vessels.

Based on the successful developments in other industries, this provides an insight into how the liner shipping industry will be handling pricing, booking uptake and capacity management in 2025. The underlying premise for this to be successful within a shipping line is the ability to be able to control and manage the internal processes, as also outlined in the section on process management. Embarking on an effort to improve yield management without contemplating process management is likely to result in failure – or at best a substantially reduced effect.

Different methodologies and systems are available, and shipping lines are likely to develop their own internal systems and processes which will all differ somewhat. However the core dynamics will be along the following lines:

The core will be the existence of an integrated database where all relevant data pertaining to bookings, prices and capacity is available. This includes the location and availability of containers in depots, the availability of feeder capacity, both own and 3rd party as well as capacity restrictions in ports.

The starting point is the presence of a back-bone network. The dynamics for designing this network will be covered in the next chapter. Given the back-bone network, the objective is to maximize profitability given this network.

Part of the designing the back-bone network includes medium to long term forecasting of overall demand flows, and is used to establish initial allocation of capacity on the vessels.

The allocation of costs to arrive at underlying unit costs becomes a matter of choice for the individual shipping line, where different methodologies can be applied. Which methodology is chosen is less relevant – the relevant part is that the shipping line needs to analyse how the choice will impact the decision-making processes, and whether there is alignment between the drivers resulting from the cost allocation and the intention built into the processes. If there is not an alignment, the shipping line will have to change either the cost allocation or the processes.

Having made this setup, it becomes critical to leverage the real-time data as well as the forecasting of endogenous parameters. This should be used to continuously balance pricing changes with capacity re-allocation, striving to maximize both vessel utilization and revenue. This is best illustrated with a simple example.

Assume a vessel is sailing on the following rotation: Busan – Shanghai – Hong Kong- Singapore – Rotterdam. For simplicity we can assume the vessel has a capacity of 16.000 TEU, and the carrier has planned to load 4.000 TEU from each of the Asian ports. It is initially expected that the freight rate out of each port is 1000 USD/TEU.

The shipping line will continuously monitor the booking uptake at each port, and match the actual uptake curve with the expected uptake curve.

The expected uptake curve is a combination of spot cargo and expected contractual cargo. Given the current market status of bookings being made but not showing up, the shipping line will be planning for an uptake curve which targets more than 4.000 TEU from each of the ports. As we progress toward 2025, the amount of enforceable contracts will gradually increase, making it possible for the shipping lines to plan and forecast the uptake curves with increasing accuracy.

Whenever the actual booking uptake does not match the expected uptake, this is a signal to the shipping line that they need to take active action. First of all they will investigate what the reason is for the deviation. Fundamentally the deviation can be due to two very different factors.

One factor is a shift in market share whereby the shipping line is either gaining or losing market share. The other factor is a change in the underlying market resulting in either higher or lower total volumes, in turn impacting the actual uptake curve.

Presently it is almost impossible for shipping lines to ascertain whether they are subjected to one or the other of these factors, and the underlying problem here is the lack of transparency pertaining to the demand flows in the market. As covered in the previous chapter, it should be expected that such levels of transparency will become available over the coming decade. Therefore the shipping lines' yield management process will be able to distinguish between these two factors.

Separating these two are essential in order to maximize revenue given that it is a zero-sum game. Not being able to separate is likely to lead to value-destroying decisions. If the booking uptake is slower than expected this is either due to the market being weak or a competitor gaining market share. If we initially contemplate only pricing as a tool with which to change the uptake curve, it is easy to see the difference. If the driver is competitive action, then the lowering of prices might be an appropriate tactical counter-measure to regain the lost market share.

However, if the underperformance is due to a weaker market, the use of pricing as a tool will be highly detrimental. In this case the shipping line can only gain volume at the expense of other shipping lines – and in this case the other shipping lines are also experiencing a shortfall due to the lower market. If they now begin to lose market share on top of this, they will be prompted into pricing action as well and a rapid downward pricing spiral will ensue. If all carriers are equally adept, the net result will be that everyone maintain their existing market share but at a substantially reduced rate level. No-one will be able to elevate their booking uptake curve to match their planned vessel utilization.

Hence the action which might be appropriate in one situation can be highly detrimental in another – even though the booking uptake curves are identical. This further underscores why the shipping lines in 2025 will all have implemented yield management processes and systems. If only a few shipping lines are doing this – and indeed a few are quite far down this path already - anyone not doing so would have a significant competitive disadvantage.

Conversely, of course, if the booking uptake is stronger than anticipated. In this case the carrier can due increase pricing to the point where demand is reduced to match capacity. In such an instance, it is less relevant whether the strong uptake is due to the market or to competitive action as the relevant action – a price increase – is the same.

But with yield management, the point is that pricing is not the only tool to be used. Staying with the example from above, assume the booking uptake curve for the first port in the rotation, Busan, indicate that the shipping line will only get 3.000 TEU of bookings. At this point such a development should be cross-checked with the booking uptake curves in the subsequent ports. It might be that the uptake curve for Shanghai indicates bookings of 5.000 TEU. In this case the shipping line abstains from using pricing as a tool and instead re-allocates the capacity on the vessel accordingly. The net result being a full vessel at no price change.

Of course, reality becomes more complicated. The pricing elasticity in Shanghai might well deviate from that in Busan leading to further changes in the re-allocation. The changes in both Busan and Shanghai might be driven by a combination of market developments and competitor actions. Additionally, there might not be a sufficient stock of empty containers available in Shanghai to manage a full re-allocation, or the types of containers needed might be different than what is in stock. The list of such details becomes quite substantial once a shipping line begins to plan for this. However, this is where the combination of process management and advanced computer models will provide the necessary support. Some might see such systems and analysis as "Big Data", but the key here is that the dataflow and analysis has to be designed from a process perspective, and not from the perspective of using a Big Data approach to find correlations in the data.

But this approach also has other process-related implications which the carriers will have to adapt to over the coming years.

In terms of managing the sales force, the dynamic re-allocation of capacity across geographies will make it difficult to operate with traditional sales targets, especially for spot cargo. A sales person might be performing perfectly well, but due to a sudden market strength in a port 2000 miles away, he finds that his allocation is being reduced – making it impossible for him to meet a previously set volume or revenue target. Whilst traditional sales targets could still be used for larger, enforceable, contracts, this will not be the case for spot cargo. Consequently we will see the shipping lines undergo a change in their approach towards sales management centered around yield optimization rather than local volume or revenue.

The people responsible for setting price levels in the shipping lines will also see a change with the advent of yield management and real-time data. As we have already seen previously, part of the challenge is the transparency which will be entering the market. However, this transparency in the spot market can equally well be used to become better at setting the correct price. Other industries have over the past decade become extremely skilled at using online sales platforms as a means to fine-tune pricing. By performing analysis on the behaviour of online clients, it is possible to forecast price sensitivities and price points much more accurately than what the current manual process in the shipping lines are capable of. Furthermore, having the ability to differentiate pricing between enforceable and non-enforceable contracts and spot cargo will provide the shipping lines with another tool to optimize pricing.

Action Point: Yield Management

To re-emphasize the point already made, harnessing yield management is already possible using existing technology. For the shipping lines the main challenge towards 2025 is not as much the development of the systems – although it should not be seen as simple matter – it is the development and implementation of well-defined and structured processes encompassing pricing, sales and capacity management. This transition will, realistically, take several years to accomplish for a shipping line which commits to it. This in turn means that a shipping line which is not convinced that this is needed, will find themselves in an untenable position once several competitors have completed their transformations.

It should also be clear that commissioning an IT system before contemplating the necessary process changes, is unlikely to be successful.

Finally, it must be recognized that once the development of integrated yield management processes is initiated, it will quickly encompass multiple adjacent processes such as equipment management, feeder management, tendering for large clients, surcharge and free-time policies etc. This underscores the point made earlier, the process management in general is a pivotal exercise for shipping lines in their development towards 2025.

Key questions:

How do you plan to improve the processes and systems related to cost recognition in order to integrate real time data into commercial decision processes?

How do you manage the forecast of exogenous parameters, and do you allow internal non-experts to override the forecast of exogenous parameters?

How to you plan to integrate quantifiable data with unstructured data based on feedback from customers?

How do you plan to improve the real-time monitoring and forecasting of booking uptake curves?

How do you plan to integrate the pricing, sales and capacity management processes?

How do you plan to use online pricing as a means to improve price discovery?

How do you plan to manage the sales force in an environment of dynamic re-allocation of capacity?

The Complexities of Network Design

The current liner shipping networks are the results of 40 years of increasing vessel sizes, necessitating the build-up of hub-and-spoke operations. In essence there has been one overarching driving force: unit costs. Very simply, a larger vessel results in a lower cost per container, or per slot-mile produced. The high sustained growth rates in the market allowed shipping lines to continuously increase the size of new vessels, while still be able to absorb the added capacity.

But whilst it is clear, that the unit costs for a container on a specific vessel is subject to clear scale advantages as the vessel size grows, the relationship becomes much more complex if the focus is shifted to the cost of the entire network.

In a complex shipping network, the usage of large vessels might result in a high incidence of costly transhipments, whereas smaller vessels would provide more direct port-port services. This would result in higher unit costs for the vessel operations, but reduce the costs of transhipment and local feedering services. The calculation of the optimal situation is not always straight forward, and it can change significantly when especially oil prices and charter rates for vessels change.

But the complexity of the network itself makes it difficult to change at short notice. The presence of major transhipment hubs in the network results in a situation where it is difficult to make a smaller network change without impacting multiple other services. Additionally, making a major network redesign is complicated by the practicalities of having to re-negotiate agreements with a large range of terminals. Adding to this is the complexity of different interests within an alliance where different terminals interests and customer groups might not be aligned.

A network consists of what can be termed the back-bone network which is the deployment patterns of the major vessels on deep-sea routes connecting hubs as well as major ports. In addition to this, is has a large range of more localized niche and feeder services.

Given the aforementioned complexities, fundamental changes to the back-bone network does not happen frequently. Consequently, the design of the backbone network has to be seen as the core decision within a shipping line, and the foundation upon which the yield management processes need to rest.

Presently the design of the core network in many shipping lines is not subjected to any advanced mathematical modelling, however this will change towards 2025.

Part of the reason for the current status is that networks have evolved gradually over time, and therefore the current designs are often the result of work performed by highly skilled individuals who have, quite literally, been doing this from the point in time where the networks were extremely simple. They have a solid intuitive understanding of the inner workings of their networks. This, however, presents the liner shipping companies with two challenges.

One challenge is related to training of new people. Having been part of a process over 20-40 years wherein the networks have gradually grown is not something a new employee can be taken through. Whilst particularly gifted individuals might indeed appear, it is unlikely to anticipate that shipping lines can take in new employees to the network design departments and train them to intuitively understand the intricacies of the complex global networks.

This lead us to the second challenge. What happens instead, is that the new employees will get a solid understanding of individual components of the network and focus on optimizing these components. But the ramifications of changes in one part of the network on another part might simply elude such an approach. It is the quintessential example of the butterfly effect where the flapping of the wings of a butterfly in Hawaii will result in a Typhoon in Hong Kong.

Given the fact the analytical tools have already been developed within which to model the full complexities, and that such tools are being used, it also becomes clear that scientific modelling of the complexities of a network will have become the standard by 2025.

In order to ensure optimization of the network, such tools combine the three key elements which are at the heart of a successful network: Cost and operational aspects of deploying vessels, the ability to actually carry the planned cargo for the customers and finally the ability to reposition the surplus empty containers through the network.

The technological development will ensure that such tools will become increasingly sophisticated and contain an increasing amount of details and modelling capabilities. But, as also seen in other critical elements, the main change for the shipping lines lie in the underlying approach to the process itself.

First of all, carriers will be seeing the design of the network as the basis upon which their commercial and operational process will rest. This is due to the simple fact that the network is the element which takes the longest time to change. As the markets are constantly in development, it is not realistic to expect the networks to change in response to such tactical changes. Instead the yield management processes need to bridge the gap between the network and any minor market deviations.

Apart from shifting into advanced mathematical modelling, the network design will be centered around four core principles, with different shipping lines lending different weight to each point.

The design needs to be resilient. This means that the same back-bone network needs to remain efficient in the face of market changes over an extended period of time.

The design needs to ensure the utilization of the largest vessels. The class of 18-21.000 TEU vessels is not only the most costly assets for the shipping lines, it is also the least flexible assets. Hence any back-bone network needs to adopt the most efficient usage of these assets.

The design needs to maximize the synergies between the shipping line and any terminal ownership they might have in ports associated with the network.

The design needs to meet customer requirements.

The requirement of resilience is necessary. As the networks grow larger and more complex, it becomes increasingly difficult to make major changes quickly. Therefore, the network need to be able to withstand changes such as customer composition, changes in market growth, fluctuations in oil price etc. resilience can be tested by having a comprehensive model of the network and simulate a range of external impacts. Not only will this allow to quantify the level of resilience in the network but it will also allow the shipping lines to set trigger points for action. If identified trigger points are reached, this indicates that the network must now undergo a change in order to remain efficient.

The issue with the vessels is a consequence of the deliveries of the mega vessels in the period 2013-2018. These represent a sizeable investment, and with an expected lifespan of 25 years it is not realistic to assume these vessels will be scrapped or idled. The problem is, that the demographic development in combination with the trends towards near shoring will tend to disperse the trade volumes.

From a network design perspective, large vessels are optimal in a situation of concentrated trade flows between a limited range of major locations. But the overall trends pointing toward 2025 are the opposite of this. Hence the logical conclusion is that the networks which will be designed by the major shipping lines will not necessarily be optimal seen purely from the perspective of the trade flows – but they will be optimal given the constraint that the largest vessel must be used.

Finally there is the aspect of the terminals. As is outlined in the later section pertaining to the impact on terminals, we are likely to enter a period where substantial overcapacity will emerge. However, due to consolidation of shipping lines, both by mergers and by alliances, this overcapacity will impact in a highly uneven fashion. Some terminals will experience increased growth, whereas other are at risk of severe declines. Who will be the winners in this game will to a high degree be determined in the shipping lines' process for network design.

Therefore, we will see a clear pattern emerge whereby shipping lines will favour network designs which might appear less efficient, but at the same time ensures volumes through terminals in which they have ownership stakes.

The fourth parameter is the need to meet customer requirements. It is not a coincidence that this is listed as the last item. That does not mean that customer preferences are irrelevant, but it does signal that major shipping lines – and alliances – can only include customer preferences in a very limited fashion when designing the networks.

It is clear, that almost no matter how large a customer is, he will never account for more than a relatively small fraction of the cargo on board a vessel on the back-bone network. This in itself makes it impossible to design the main network based on individual customer preferences. Such individualized services is the realm of niche carriers or services, but not to be seen in the back-bone network.

However this does not mean that overall service parameters do not come into play. During the network design phase shipping lines will have to choose how to weight the importance of key parameters such as transit times, service frequency and the ratio of direct versus hub-and-spoke services. Given the nature of each of these three parameters it is not possible to optimize on all elements at the same time, and therein lies an opportunity for the major shipping lines to create a competitive difference.

Action Point: Network Design

By 2025, or likely quite a while prior to that, the practical mechanics of network design for the major shipping lines will be handled by mathematical algorithms. These will ensure consistency between the operational back-bone of the network, the ability to carry the targeted cargo as well as the ability to reposition empty equipment.

The design of the network will serve as a centre point for the yield management processes, with the yield management processes having the role of managing market changes in the face of a more static back-bone network.

At the same time, the back-bone network will be the subject of simulations of market variations, identifying specific trigger points which will result in changes to the back-bone network.

Due to investment decisions already performed in the industry, the network design for major shipping lines in 2025 will partially depend on the utilization of vessels and terminals, even when this is not necessarily optimal. Herein of course lies an opportunity for smaller niche players.

Key questions:

How do you plan to model the network?

How to you plan to identify trigger points for major network changes?

How to you plan to calculate the trade-off between using specific terminals versus a more optimal network design?

How to you plan to calculate the trade-off between using specific vessels versus a more optimal network design?

How do you plan to handle network design as a negotiation between alliance partners?

Implications of consolidation

2015-16 saw the largest wave of consolidation in the liner shipping industry since the inception of the industry itself. In essence, 8 out of 20 global shipping lines will be disappearing – although a few of these are still awaiting regulatory approval at the time of writing.

However, even though the sudden boost appears highly significant, it is neither unexpected nor does it in reality represent a deviation from the long-term developments. The liner shipping industry has seen a persistent drive towards consolidation for more than 30 years, and this is a drive which will continue until 2025 – however at that point the wave of consolidation will have been completed and the industry will enter into a different era.

Before we delve further into the matter of consolidation, it should be made clear that "consolidation" is not a singular phenomenon applicable only to the large shipping lines. It also applies to smaller regional and niche lines as well as to the various constellations of alliances. All of these will undergo changes in the coming years and reach a new "plateau" in 2025.

We will start by looking at the consolidation amongst the large global shipping lines. In 1996 the 10 largest shipping lines controlled 48% of the global capacity. By 2006 this had increased to 64% and by the end of 2016, including the expected mergers which had been announced, this stood at 83%. A similar progression is visible if either the broader top-20 group of carriers, or the more narrow top-5 group of carriers is considered.

This progression shows that despite the headlines pertaining to the historic wave of consolidation in 2015-16, the pace of consolidation is actually well in line with the long-term developments. The only notable aspect is that this long-term progression appears to happen more in sudden jumps and less as a slow and steady progression.

Another notable aspect of the consolidation is to calculate the Herfindahl-Hirschmann Index (HHI) for the industry. The HHI is a measure of market concentration, and, as a benchmark, the competition authorities under the US Department of Justice regards an industry with an HHI above 2500 as highly concentrated and an industry with an HHI between 1500-2500 as moderately concentrated.

In 1996 the HHI for the global liner shipping industry was 330 indicating a highly fragmented industry. In 2006 the HHI stood at 660 and by the end of 2016 – including the expected mergers – the HHI had increased to a level of 1000. Not only does this, again, confirm the steady progression of consolidation over a long period of time, it also shows that the industry remains fragmented.

One of the barriers which has prevented stronger consolidation in the industry has been the ownership structure of many main shipping lines. They have tended to be majority owned by either nation states or family-controlled entities, most of which have had little inclination to divest of their shipping lines, while at the same time having the ability to attract additional funding in challenging times. That Hanjin was the first major global shipping ever to go bankrupt in 2016 is testament to the willingness, and ability, of the owners to keep the lines operating independently.

As the market continues to become commoditized – driven both by the need to achieve scale advantages as well as the digitization and automation trends – the market concentration is highly likely to increase further, as increased market concentration is a predeterminant for improved profitability. Due to competition legislation the market concentration cannot increase indefinitely, and hence it is expected that the end point of the drive towards industry concentration will be at a level of 6-8 main global shipping lines. Furthermore it is expected that this level will be reached by 2025 in line with the long-term trend of consolidation.

Given the consolidation round which is presently ongoing, this will leave 11-12 major global players depending on how one defines "major global" players, and hence the expectation is for some 3-5 of these to disappear over the coming decade. Which ones they will be, remains an open question. Due to the ownership structures mentioned previously, the competitive landscape involves state sponsored actors as well as actors with access to substantial funds outside the core business of the shipping company itself.

However, it is becoming clear that this group of global shipping lines is being separated into ultra-large large shipping lines and lines which are "merely" large global carriers. With the implementation of the new alliance structures in 2017, this has provided an environment wherein virtually all the major global shipping lines are insulated against major strategic threats for the coming years. Before progressing further on the ramifications of this, it is necessary to examine the role of the alliances within the context of consolidation.

Alliances are operational entities providing scale advantages for the shipping lines. They provide some of the advantages of mergers, but not all of them, and also come with a set of disadvantages.

Most importantly, the alliances are by law forbidden to coordinate commercial activities. Carriers within an alliance may not discuss or coordinate pricing, marketing or any other commercial activity. They are in all commercial aspects to compete and not to collaborate.

The purpose of the alliances is to generate operational scale advantages. One source of scale advantage stems from the vessel size, as we have already seen earlier. What an alliance allows is the creation of scale advantages as well as flexibility within a network. As a very simple example consider 4 shipping lines each providing a weekly service between Asia and Europe. They all cover cargo from 10 ports in Asia to

10 ports in Europe. A total of 100 port-pairs to service. Each shipping line may have chosen to only call 5 ports in either region in order to have competitive transit times. As a consequence, each shipping line covers 25 ports pairs directly, and have to use local feeders and associated transhipments to cover the remaining 75 port pairs. If the 4 shipping lines enter into an alliance they can collectively design a network comprised of 4 weekly services, now with the option to provide a direct port-port service for any of the 100 port-port pairs. Each carrier still operates the same vessels, but they will all save the feeder and transhipment costs. The is a cost advantage related to the scale of the network instead of the scale of the vessels.

This alliance of 4 shipping lines could also have chosen to expand the service frequency on some ports, or chose of cover some ports with both fast and slow products. Additionally they could have chosen to replace their existing vessels with slightly larger vessels and operate only 3 weekly services, reaping the scale benefits of the larger vessels.

The scale of the alliance creates opportunities for network design which none of the carriers have on their own. This is the key benefit of the alliances. The actual benefits are highly dependent on the exact deployment patterns, vessels and terminals used, however modelling of generic alliance set-ups have shown that the cost advantages related to network scale are as substantial for an entire alliance as the cost advantages related to the increased vessel is for an individual carrier.

This also has the implication that with the current market structure it is not feasible for any individual carrier to operate their own back-bone network and be competitive relative to a large alliance. Looking forward to 2025, and the consolidation which is expected by then, it also implies that even in 2025 we will see alliance structures in operation. Essentially there are three possible scenarios for 2025.

One scenario has the markets dominated by three major alliances – similar to the situation which come into place in 2017. The reason being that competition authorities are highly unlikely to approve a structure with only two alliances controlling the market.

The other scenario is a structure wherein mergers and acquisitions have resulted in one shipping line becoming substantially larger than the other shipping lines. In this case the large shipping line might choose to operate independently, but this would result in the other shipping lines coalescing around two major alliances in order to provide competitive networks.

The third scenario is a market with no alliances. This scenario will not develop as a result of market forces, as the emergence of such a structure would increase costs for all shipping lines and reduce their operational flexibility. However, the reason for mentioning this scenario is in case competition authorities decide to eliminate the use of alliances on account of pressure from shipper groups.

Given these scenarios, the most likely outcome is the first scenario encompassing three main alliances. As the market commoditization is likely to gradually expand from the main east-west trades to other large, and growing, deep-sea trades, the geographical scope of the alliances is likely to expand as well.

It is therefore clear that alliances provide significant benefits. However, they also give rise to two main disadvantages.

The difference in commercial priorities between alliance members, combined with different levels of terminal involvement makes it difficult to develop an optimal network design. The alliances will gradually begin to employ mathematical modelling tools, as outlined in the previous chapter on network design. However with multiple carriers present, the models will have to take more constraints into account in order to reach a compromise between the members. Hence, all else being equal, there will be a correlation between the efficiency of the network and the number of alliance members. Additionally, the need for alliance members to agree on changes to the network design will result in a reduced capability in responding to rapid market changes.

An even more severe disadvantage of the alliance is the commercial implication. Because of the anti-trust legislation, alliance members are competing directly for cargo which will be loaded on the exact same vessels. Hence for a shipper who has chosen to use a specific alliance, the port-port ocean part operated by the alliance is a pure commodity, leaving the alliance members open for pricing arbitrage. Incidentally, this is in itself another reason why we will see the emergence of online-priced transactional products during the coming decade, as the shipping lines are forced to find a solution to this self-imposed commoditization of part of their product.

This brings us back to the consolidation amongst the major carriers. With the emergence of the 3-alliance structure, mergers and acquisitions will be much simpler, and less risky, to carry out amongst carriers within the same alliance. Mergers of shipping lines in different alliances will cause a re-shuffling of the alliances as a shipping line cannot be a member of multiple alliances. As an example, the coming 3-alliance structure was triggered by the mergers of COSCO and CSCL as well as between CMA CGM and APL, both of which operated in different alliances.

The likely scenario to unfold will therefore be the implementation of the new structure in 2017, with alliance members seeking to create some semblance of market stability during 2018-2020 as the structural imbalance in the market is gradually brought under control. However, at some point there will be a trigger event where one of the current major shipping lines will be sold – either because the owners decide that it is a good time and/or price to sell at, or because it is last resort to avoid a bankruptcy. If this happens between two carriers from different alliances, it is highly likely to lead to a re-shaping of the alliances, and in that process additional mergers are likely to happen, similarly to the dynamic that evolved rapidly in 2016.

In conclusion this leads to the most likely scenario being a market wherein the global, commoditized, deep-sea trades are dominated by 6-8 major shipping lines organized in 3 alliances.

In this context it should be kept in mind that alliances are merely large and complex versions of the smaller vessel sharing agreements shipping lines make with each other on essentially all trades globally.

Hence the market outside the commoditized deep-sea trades in 2025 will continue to see vessel sharing agreements both between major global shipping lines from different alliances – as the alliances would remain the domain of the commoditized markets – as well as between major global shipping lines and regional niche lines.

This brings us to a view at the development of the niche liners towards 2025 which will be covered in the next section. But before then, what are the key points to focus on for the main shipping lines?

Action Point: Consolidation

By 2025, the dynamics for the deep-sea trades will have seen further consolidation to the point where we have 6-8 main global carriers, likely organized in 3 main alliances.

The main back-bone products of the main lines individually as well as for the alliances will be principally designed from the perspective of maximizing the value of their assets – i.e. principally vessels and terminals.

Key questions:

Do you plan to become a shipping line who acquires another line to e amongst the 6-8 prevailing lines, or do you plan to be acquired?

If you plan to be the acquirer, will you target a member of your own alliance, and thereby gradually build into the acquisition? Or do you plan to acquire a line from a different alliance forcing a disruption in the competitors' setup?

How do you build the strength to become the acquirer?

If you do not plan to become the acquirer, how do you build the strongest possible platform for a sale, and what that sale look like?

How do you plan to alleviate the planning inefficiencies inherent in an alliance?

How do you prefer your alliance constellation to expand beyond its current scope?

The Niche Carriers

As we have seen the dynamics for the major shipping lines will be governed by the adaptation of scale advantages, commoditization and digitization. But the dynamics will on some of these parameters be different for the niche carriers.

First it should be made clear that "niche" carrier is to be understood in a relative broad sense. With the market developments towards 2025, a niche carrier in this context is in essence any carrier which is not amongst the small group of ultra-large global shipping lines.

The reason all the remaining shipping lines rightfully can be called niche carriers is that they will have to compete in an environment where it will be impossible to match the main lines on the commoditized main products that they deliver. But this does not mean there is no scope for them to compete – quite the opposite in fact. For each of the main advantages that the main shipping lines have, i.e. scale, standardization and digitization, let us explore how these can be used as strengths for well-adapted niche carriers as well.

On the aspect of scale, we have already seen how this applies both to vessel sizes and network reach. On the face of it, that would seem difficult for the niche carriers to compete with, but reality turns out to be different.

First of all, though, it should be kept in mind that the niche lines do have a sizeable potential upside from using larger vessels. In fact their relative upside is much more significant than for the big shipping lines. Upsizing from a 15.000 TEU vessel to an 18.000 TEU will provide a much smaller relative unit cost saving than the upsizing from an 800 TEU to a 1200 TEU vessel. As always, the unit costs savings are only realised if the larger vessels can be filled. This in turn leads to the logical conclusion that we will indeed see an increase in consolidation amongst the niche carriers as well, simply in order to attain these scale efficiencies.

Additionally, the ownership structures are not as rigid for all niche carriers as they are for the major shipping lines. This means that it is a segment where it is not uncommon to see carriers go bankrupt. This implies that the consolidation in the niche segment will take place not only through mergers and acquisitions – as is the case for the major shipping lines – but also through organic growth resulting in some carriers folding.

In this context it must be noted that some of the main shipping lines have chosen strategies where they are the owners of minor niche carriers – or niche brands depending on perspective. Most prominently at the beginning of 2017 are Maersk Line's ownership of Safmarine, Seago, MCC Transport, SeaLand and Mercosul with Hamburg Süd and CCNI to be added, as well as CMA CGM's ownership of APL, ANL, Cheng Lie Navigation, Feeder Associate System, Cagema, MacAndrews, OPDR and CoMaNav.

This implies that some of the main shipping lines have reached the conclusion that these local niche carriers have an ability to address a segment of the market which the main shipping line itself cannot do as efficiently.

In turn, this means that the consolidation we will see amongst the niche carriers will also be influenced by the desire by the main shipping lines to increase their reach into these markets.

Whereas a specific forecast could be made of the number of main global shipping lines the market would have in 2025, this is not feasible in the same way for the niche carriers – with a single exception for feeder carriers as we shall touch on shortly. The reason is that the barrier of entry for small niche carriers is relatively low, and especially when the market is in a down cycle where assets can be chartered at extremely low rates, this can make it attractive for newcomers. Going

129

forward, over capacity at the ports and terminals will further lower the barriers of entry. Finally, as we shall also touch upon, digitization also provides a significant opportunity – perhaps more for newcomers than for more established niche lines.

If we initially focus on the specific market for feedering services, this is clearly a specific niche within the container shipping markets. In this context we are purely contemplating the shipment of containers on behalf of other shipping lines, typically connecting smaller outports with larger transhipment hubs.

This is a market where there are significant scale advantages of a nature which differs from the scale advantages enjoyed by the main container shipping lines. In addition to the same scale advantages – vessel size and network breadth – which applies to the main carriers, the ability to pool cargo from multiple carriers and reduce the volatility of volume is a significant effect. As feeder services cater for cargo to smaller outports, this has two major ramifications. The volume of cargo to each port is relatively limited, and due to the limited volume of cargo, the fluctuations in cargo volume can become quite significant. As a very simple example consider two main shipping lines who compete for cargo destined for a small outport. Every other week each shipping line succeed in re-capturing the cargo from the competitor. Each shipping line therefore experience a very high volatility in volume each week. If each shipping line operate their own small feeder service to the outport in question, this service will be severely underutilized 50% of the time. If, instead, the cargo was moved by a 3rd party feeder operator, who had both of the main lines as clients, the feeder operator would experience a stable cargo flow, as the same cargo needs to be moved – the only thing which changes from week to week is the name of the main shipping line who has the main contract. The net effect would be that the vessel utilization increased overall, and the cost in the system would be reduced.

Other similar "hidden" effects are associated with 3rd party feeder services to smaller outports. Notably the ability to cater for volatile empty equipment repositioning, the ability to have multiple weekly services which drastically reduces the impact of delays and lay-overs in the main transhipment hubs as well as the ability for main shipping lines to see local feedering services as purely variable costs. SeaIntel Maritime Analysis have previously analysed the economic value pool associated with these "hidden" value pools and concluded that the value pool purely for Europe amounts to a quarter billion USD annually versus a situation where the main shipping lines primarily focus on providing their own feeder services.

As the main shipping lines, who are the potential main beneficiaries of this value pool, continue to embark on the usage of better mathematical modelling tools for both the back-bone network and for the tactical use of yield management systems, the amount of feedering cargo handled by 3rd party feeders, instead of the main shipping lines themselves, will increase. Additionally, as the value pool is strongly linked to the size of the network offered by the feeder carrier – i.e. both the number of outports served as well as the frequency of services to those outports, we will see a development where a few 3rd party feeders will be gaining a scale that will hard for competitors to match. Clearly there are nuances, but from a macro-perspective the important parts are feedering in Asia, Europe and the Americas. Whilst in theory one could see different feeder lines be successful in each of the areas, it is highly likely that the same feeder lines will come to dominate in all three areas. This is simply due to the ability to leverage the know-how of the individual successful feeder line as well as the relationship which will be developed between a feeder line and a main shipping line – who by definition will have a need for feeder services in all geographies.

Hence, the leads to a situation where we are likely to see 2-3 main niche carriers dominate the 3rd party feedering market by 2025. Theoretically one 3rd party feeder could reduce the overall costs even further, however the main shipping lines are highly unlikely to allow a situation to develop wherein their feedering needs will become subject to a monopolistic entity. Hence, from a strategic point of view, they would continue to provide sufficient volume to have at least 2 major feeder operators. Additionally, as the market is likely dominated by 3 major alliances in 2025, each alliance might weight their usage of feeders differently, hence leaving space for three main 3rd party feeders.

A feeder operator furthermore has a choice whether to be a pure feeder operator – i.e. only move containers controlled by other carriers – or carry a mix between feeder cargo and short-sea cargo, where the short-sea cargo consists of containers shipped directly on behalf of cargo owners or freight forwarders. Both approaches have their merits, and we are likely to continue to see both models being used. The pure feeder carrier have the advantage of an extremely simple commercial set-up. They have very few customers – the carriers – and hence they have no need for an extended sales or customer service division. This also means that they can be seen as fully neutral in relation to the main shipping lines. On the other hand, the feeder carrier who also accepts short-sea cargo can increase their volumes, and use the increased volume to leverage their scale even further by increasing both vessel sizes and the breadth of the network.

Now we will turn our attention to those niche carriers who are not predominantly feeder carriers.

For these niche carriers there is a range of options available, but at the same time the overall developments will place parts of the existing business models under severe pressure.

First there is the strategic imperative to increase the vessel sizes being used. This is a development which has accelerated during 2015-2016, as the availability of cheap large assets has grown. Furthermore, the introduction of global low-Sulphur rules by 2020 will result in a situation where fuel costs will increase significantly, further enhancing the savings of larger vessels. In essence the "game" for larger vessels amongst the niche players is no different than the "game" played by the main shipping lines. The main difference being that the smaller niche carriers can, and occasionally do, indeed go bankrupt. As the niche carriers are exchanging smaller vessels for larger vessels, this de-facto results in a significant injection of capacity in the trades they serve. Often niche carriers only have a single service in a specific trade, and hence cannot compensate for the injection of vessel capacity by reducing service frequency. During 2016 alone this led to a capacity growth amongst the niche carriers which was more than three times higher than the global demand growth. Such a development will quickly prove to be unsustainable. The inevitable consequence will be the removal of some niche carriers, and therefore consolidation.

But, unlike the situation for the main global shipping lines, the barriers of entry are quite low for a niche service, and therefore it is not possible to predict the number of niche services. If the very smallest of local services are included, the number will remain very high – but the degree of concentration as measured by the HHI index will climb, and in each individual local trade we are likely see a reduction to just a handful of operators at most.

The coming digitization and automation is both a threat and an opportunity for the niche carriers. On one hand it is a clear threat. The smaller shipping lines do not have the budgets the major lines have to drive this development, and therefore they are likely to be behind the curve on IT and systems development. On the other hand, precisely because of this problem, there is a market for the development of generic digitization and automation services for the niche carriers, and it is likely that 3rd party vendors will be stepping into this space. These can either be established vendors in the industry – most likely existing portals – or entirely new entities who will develop these services with the mindset which has driven digitization in other industries, free of the conventional mindset of the shipping lines themselves.

A local niche carrier who is able to combine a cost-efficient generic digitization and automation drive with local knowledge for customers whose business is more complex, and hence cannot be fully automated, can be powerful. Similarly, a local niche carrier might be able to leverage the local knowledge with the flexibility associated with their small size to provide online digitized solutions that are competitive in specific segments of the market.

Despite the significant value inherent in digitization and automation, niches also will remain wherein it is possible to thrive without these tools. The niches will not be large, but where they do exist, they might be quite profitable. These are niches where either local trading conditions, or laws, prevent services from being fully digitized, or tailor-made agreements with specific clients to service their specific needs. These types of agreements might indeed constitute regular liner services on paper, but will de-facto more resemble the individual agreements known from the tramper trades.

The global transparency of services and prices which is forthcoming will allow niche operators to analyse the full spectrum of services in the market and not only identify specific gaps which are not serviced, but also leverage the digitization to make their own services visible to a vast range of clients. This means, that we are likely to continue to see niche services appear, even within the otherwise commoditized deep-sea trades, as the niche carriers tap into specific needs of relatively small customer groups. These will be services predominantly focused on aspects such as speed and reliability. Both from the positive and the negative angle. Due to the sheer size of vessels they need to fill, the main shipping lines are unable to fill an entire vessel with cargo which all needs a very fast speed. However, a niche carrier deploying a much smaller vessel can conceivable do this, in turn competing with, for example, overland or sea-air solutions. Likewise, a niche carrier might launch a concept where the transit time is very long, maybe even undetermined, in exchange for quite low freight rates. The exact nature and amount of such niche services is impossible to predict, however it is clear that in the marketplace of 2025 we will see a solid place for small niche carriers who are able to adapt to the new reality. But it is equally likely that many of the smaller niche carriers today will quite simply disappear if they do not adjust their current models to the new reality.

A final important aspect pertaining to the niche carriers is that in some geographies they are not subjected to the same zero-sum game as the main shipping lines are. In some local trades, the cargo can flow either by sea or by land, and this creates a dynamic where changes in the relative competitiveness between the transportation modes will result in changes in the underlying shipment volumes as well. Hence for the niche carriers there is the added possibility to improve competitiveness versus land side transportation, and in turn increase volumes. In most, but not all, geographies, land-based transportation is clearly faster than ocean transportation. This can be partly reduced by having access to more frequent shipping services, but at the end of the day there will still be a difference in transit time. But one element which will change is the complexity associated with using shipping services. In many places the documentation processes associated with using shipping services can be substantially more cumbersome than using land based transportation. When this is combined with cargo owners who are used to using land based transportation, this presents a formidable barrier. However, as digitization and automation progresses, this competitive difference between short sea shipping and land-based transportation will gradually be eliminated towards 2025.

Action Point: Niche Carriers

By 2025, substantial consolidation will have happened between the current niche players in general, and for feeder services in particular.

Furthermore, we will have seen the emergence of new types of niche carriers specialized in leveraging their local expertise with the transparency of the digitized container markets – both to analyse niche opportunities as well as to leverage the ability to reach a vast number of potential customers. These will be a mix of existing niche carriers who have transformed themselves and entirely new carriers which will be launched over the coming years.

Key questions:

If you are a feeder carrier, what is your plan to ensure you reach critical scale and becomes one of the 2-3 major feeder carriers in 2025?

If you are a feeder carrier, how will the digitization of the industry impact you evaluation in terms of purely having feeder cargo versus also having short sea cargo?

As a niche carrier, what will happen to your value proposition once the market becomes fully transparent?

As a niche carrier, what is your plan for digitization and automation?

As a niche carrier, what are the key sustainable strengths you will built on to counter the digitized products from the main shipping lines?

As an investor not currently in the market – how do you plan to identify gaps in the market and leverage the digitized products to your benefit?

Automation and Digitization

When automation is discussed in the context of liner shipping. it is often from the perspective of technological possibilities. It includes topics such autonomous ships, fully automated container terminals and 3D printing. This chapter will look at automation, but not from the view of a specific technology, and therefore not from the perspective of how the technology will work in detail, nor who will be developing it. Instead it will consider automation from the perspective of how it will change the dynamics and business models in the industry.

Automation is quite simply the transformation where human labour is replaced by computers or robots. When work is being replaced purely by software we would call it digitization. This is feasible for all aspects of the workflow which is related to the capturing, processing and transfer of information. When physical work is replaced by robots, this is what we will term automation.

Let us contemplate automation first. The key physical processes which are taking place within liners shipping can be broken down to consist of the following: land-side transportation, vessel operations, port operations, container stuffing and unstuffing as well as maintenance and repair of the containers. In a broader context it would involve the automation of manufacturing in general as well, as this has a direct impact on the demand flows for container transportation. Some of these aspects will be significantly impacted by automation, whereas others will result in only limited impact. Additionally, as the horizon for the outlook is 2025, some of the automation changes are unlikely to be fully implemented by that time, in which case the perspective will be expanded to go beyond 2025 as well.

Let us start with the operation of the vessels. From an automation standpoint, conceptual designs for the fully autonomous vessels have already been developed. These vessels are designed to operate with zero crew on board. From a technological perspective it is entirely plausible that even major deep-sea vessels can be constructed to be autonomous. However, from the perspective of deep-sea liner shipping it is very unlikely that this will be the case by 2025. There are essentially four key reasons for this.

The first reason is economic. The autonomous vessel has two main advantages, both linked to cost savings. One is the saving of all crew costs, and the other is operational savings as the autonomous vessel will be designed to always operate in the most efficient manner with respect to fuel consumption, schedule reliability, wear and tear on the machinery etc. Depending on the size of the vessel and its deployment patters, the actual savings pertaining to this can vary significantly.

In addition to the operational savings we will also see a significant increase in the cost of constructing the vessel. As the vessel is intended to be fully autonomous, this in turn means that there will be no crew on board to handle repair and maintenance. As long as the failures can be repaired via remote access to either software or remote controlled robots, this is not a major issue. However, a vessel operating on a deep-sea route will be exposed to conditions which can lead to mechanical breakdown of many types of equipment on board, and it is not feasible by 2025 to expect the on-board presence of robots sufficiently versatile to be able to carry out all types of repair which a human can do today.

This in turn leads to the conclusion that in order for a fully autonomous deep-sea vessel to be viable by 2025, it has to be constructed with a resilience which prevents mechanical failures while en route. Or at least eliminates failures which would prevent the vessel from reaching the next port. From a purely technological perspective this should be possible. We are already used to mechanical systems being constructed with an extremely high degree of resilience against failures – commercial airliners, satellites or pacemakers would be just a few of examples of this. But this is where the economic angle makes its appearance. Building systems to such high degrees of resilience, with multiple redundancies, would make the construction of such autonomous vessels much more expensive than traditional vessels with crew on board. Furthermore, such vessels would need a much higher degree of physical maintenance while they are in port – just as, for example, commercial airlines undergo significant mechanical tests and maintenance. This will add yet another cost component to the operation of the autonomous vessel.

The precise economic calculation of the added costs will have a very high degree of variability depending on how one chooses to forecast key elements such as the cost of building the autonomous vessel, the cost of an enhanced regime of in-port maintenance as well as the rare incidence where, against all odds, a mechanical failure does happen at sea and a repair crew has to be dispatched to fix the problem. But presently it is difficult to see that such a calculation would present a positive business case on this side of 2025. In order for the business case to be positive, we would need scale advantage both in terms of the numbers of autonomous vessels being built – to offset the expensive learning curve which is likely to come first – as well as create scale advantage for the port-side maintenance operations.

And this leads us to the second and third reasons why we are unlikely to see deep-sea liner shipping handled by autonomous vessels in 2025. This relates to the core question of whether we can trust the technology, and how quickly we can implement it if we do indeed trust it. This is a not only a question which tends to be asked in all industries, it is also a question which has been asked time and time again throughout the history of shipping. A very instructive lesson from the history of shipping is the transition from sailing ships to steam ships. Despite the superiority of the steam ships, the transition period took more than 50 years to accomplish, and this is if we only measure from the point where there was a true pick-up in the registration of new steam ships.

Whilst there were multiple reasons for this, two are important in the context of the autonomous ships as well. First there is the question of vessel reliability. A vessel owner who orders a new vessel will be investing in an asset with an expected lifespan of 25 years. He would therefore need to be convinced, that the autonomous vessel would maintain its performance for this lifespan as well – otherwise the cost of building the vessel, which will be higher than for a traditional vessels, will have to be paid off in an even shorter time span. Presently there are no such fully autonomous vessels operating, and hence there is no proven track record of a 25-year viable lifespan. Clearly the perennial chicken-and-egg situation.

Secondly, even if all vessel owners became convinced of the durability of such vessels and even if there was a clear positive economic gain, the lifespan of container vessels would act as a highly effective impediment on the construction of autonomous vessels. Given the young history of the container shipping fleet, most of the major deep-sea vessels are relatively young, and in the case of the ultra-large vessels these will all be part of the global fleet until the year 2040. The majority of existing capacity will remain in operation beyond 2025, and it is predominantly smaller vessels which are being replaced.

This in turn shows us, that if the industry is to embark on the implementation of fully autonomous vessels, this will happen with the small vessels first. In this case, the technology could be used on vessels which only serves on trades routes where they remain close to land, and hence makes it more feasible to send out a repair crew should the technology prove less resilient than planned. And for this it might well be that other vessel types than container vessels would be the first ones where the autonomous technology would be tested. Prior to any construction of larger fleets of autonomous vessels, the industry would want to evaluate the practical experienced from the first autonomous vessels.

Hence, from this perspective, the most optimistic case for autonomous vessels in liner shipping by 2025 would involve a very limited amount of vessels which would have been constructed more from the perspective of gaining experience with the technology than from the perspective of providing a superior business case. If autonomous vessels during such a trial period should prove to be feasible – not just technologically, but economically as well, the transition period from the traditional vessels is likely to be on the order of - at the very least - 25 years, matching a phase-out of vessels already in existence. This in turn means that, optimistically, the liner shipping industry would not see a firm transition to fully autonomous vessels until 2050 or beyond.

The fourth and final reason for not having autonomous vessels as part of the industry in 2025 is rooted in maritime regulations. In order to make autonomous vessels an integral part of the shipping industry, this would require upgrades of existing maritime regulations, especially the regulations pertaining to safety at sea. Whilst this can certainly be done, the speed with which such regulations are changed is not exactly staggering. As a comparison, autonomous cars are much further along their development than autonomous vessels, yet apart from permissions to perform controlled testing, no individual countries have, at the time of writing this book, developed the new laws and standards which would apply to autonomous cars. And in this case an individual country only need to agree internally on which laws should apply. For the maritime regulations to be updated in a similar fashion, all countries would essentially need to agree through a process in the IMO. Before such an agreement could be made, apart from making tests in controlled environments, the countries' representatives would want to see the results of tests. Therefore it is unlikely to expect a new maritime set of rules applying to large scale use of autonomous vessels in time for any major implementation of this by 2025.

However, this does not mean that nothing will happen to the vessels. Instead they will become semi-autonomous, which is a process that has already begun. It is a gradual process, whereby an increasing amount of each vessel's operation is being automated by retrofitting existing equipment or installing new equipment. Some operations can be taken over by computers, or the operations might remain manual but with guidance provided by computers. This eliminates the question of redundancy which is a major issue for the fully autonomous vessels as we still have crew on board to perform repairs and maintenance.

In terms of making a vessel semi-autonomous, the main savings lies in optimizing fuel consumption and minimizing wear and tear on the equipment. The installation of a vast array of sensors can be used to constantly analyse fuel consumption versus the specific operation of all mechanical equipment on board. The feedback from this analysis can be used to guide the captain to improve performance or, in realistic developments to 2025, increasingly be installed to take over operations as long as conditions at sea are calm. In order for this to function best possible, the installation of sensors is critical, as this is what allows for continuous optimization of performance. But installing sensors is not sufficient, as the data needs to be used as well. This is best accomplished in centralized computer systems, necessitating a transmission of data at very short intervals to and from the vessels.

This in turn requires a ramp-up in the availability of broadband services on the vessels. Such a ramp-up is currently happening with the launch of ever more satellites to provide such services, resulting in declining costs for satellite-based data transmissions to and from the vessels. In other words we are already seeing the rapid build-up of the data communication infrastructure which is a precursor for the semi-automation of vessel operations.

When the new low-Sulphur rules come onto effect globally from 2020, this will result in a significant increase in fuel costs for the liner shipping industry, and shipping lines will prioritise means of reducing fuel consumption even further. In the period of high fuel prices from 2010 to 2014, shipping lines spent a lot of effort in reducing fuel consumption, and were very effective at doing so. They have therefore already been able to implement many of the fuel-savings initiatives which would work in an environment of limited automation. The next big push will be the drive to semi-autonomous operations, and this is likely to be a significant part of how vessels are operated by 2025.

The ramifications of this is that the shipping lines already now need to contemplate how they are going to retrofit their existing vessels with the necessary data infrastructure and sensors, how they are going to develop programs to use the data they collect (more on that in the Big Data chapter), and how they are going to change the way the captain will be operating his vessel. This last part should not be underestimated, as the logical consequence of the semi-autonomous vessel operations is a partial removal of the autonomy of the captain.

The next part of automation is in relation to the terminals. This is a development which is already gathering significant momentum with several fully automated terminals already in operation. This is not a case of prototyping the technology, this is purely a matter of how widespread it will become, and how quickly it will happen. In addition to the fully automated terminals, the number of semi-automated terminals is increasing rapidly.

The automation of a terminal is principally directed at improving the efficiency of operations. An automated terminal can not only handle operations faster, but it makes the pace and efficiency of the operations more stable and predictable. This in turn translates into the ability to handle not only the vessels faster, but also to turn the trucks and trains faster for pick-up and drop-off. At the end of the day it creates significant efficiency savings for all stakeholders involved. In addition to the economic saving, safety and security of personnel is dramatically increased in fully automated terminals for the very simple reason that people no longer mix directly with heavy equipment. Another benefit is the ability to effectively increase the capacity of a terminal within the existing physical boundaries – something of paramount importance for terminals located in positions where additional physical expansion is not possible.

The construction of fully automated terminals is a major undertaking, and hence for many existing terminals, a semi-automated approach is more viable. This includes parts of the yards-side equipment becoming autonomous, automated equipment to handle the gate operations with the trucks, combining information received from the shipping lines with cameras which identify the trucks and containers coming into the terminal, as well as the option to have crane operators located remotely rather than physically in the cranes themselves.

The question of physical resilience is less important than it is for the vessels, as repair crews are no further away from the terminal than they have always been.

Hence, the drive toward automation, or semi-automation, has already gathered significant momentum, and by 2025 all major terminals are likely to be at semi-autonomous.

There are two main impediments to terminal automation. One is the cost of upgrading a terminal. The capital investment in automating the terminal can be substantial, and as we are headed towards a situation of terminal overcapacity in many places, this will place the profitability of many terminals under pressure, making it more difficult to find the investment funds – even though the automation is what will benefit them in the longer term.

The other impediment is the impact this will have on the port workers. Automation will result in fewer port workers. To some degree the loss of manual jobs will be replaced by other job functions needed to operate the autonomous terminals. However the total number of positions will be smaller, and the existing port workers might often not have the necessary skill set to be transferred into the new job functions which will occur. In geographical locations where labour unions are strong, this is likely to act as a delaying factor on the automation process.

Capital costs and push-back from the unions are the two key reasons why we should expect a development towards 2025 where most terminals will opt for a gradual introduction of automation rather than a sudden shift to a fully automated terminal. This means that by 2025 terminals will be in varying stages of automation, but they will all be on a path towards full automation. A terminal which is not yet highly automated should therefore contemplate not only how semi-automation can improve their operations within the next couple of years, but also contemplate when they would want to, or need to, be fully automated, and plan a path towards that goal. This way, they can avoid the problem that gradual semi-automation might leave them with equipment and systems which turn out to be incompatible when the time comes to integrate them fully. Additionally, developing a master plan towards full automation allows for the opportunity to discuss a gradual transition with local unions, thereby attempting to address the inevitable labour issues which result from automation.

An indirect impact on the liner shipping industry stems from the automation of production. Typically this is cast in the form of 3D-printing, with the concern that 3D-printing might ultimately eliminate the need for far-flung manufacturing plants. The implied consequence being a drastic reduction in shipping volumes.

However, the opposing view to this would be, that if 3-D printing does achieve the high ambitions many people have for it, it would also imply that mass-manufacturing processes would experience an equal quantum leap in production efficiency. And hence it would still be rational to concentrate manufacturing in specific locations instead of having it dispersed to every minor city in order to take advantage of these new manufacturing processes.

It would, however, also imply that the need for manufacturing to take place in very large centralized locations could be challenged, in turn dispersing production to more, mid-sized, locations. This development would be in perfect symbiosis with the demographic development outlined previously, and further underscore the challenge, that shipping companies will increasingly have to adapt to a more dispersed network as opposed to the east-west centric network.

Furthermore, the mass-production variation of the 3-D printer would more correctly be described as automated factories using robots. This is a development which is already upon us, with examples of traditional manufacturing plants previously being operated by workers in China being moved back to for example the US, where the production is now mainly performed by robots. This change does not, however, imply that the need for shipping disappears. Instead of shipping the finished products from the manufacturing plant to the outlets selling the products, there is now a need to ship the subcomponents to be used by the automated factory. This in itself reduces demand, as the subcomponents might take up less physical space than the final product, but it does not eliminate demand.

We should therefore expect the advent of automated manufacturing processes to have two effects on the liner shipping industry in 2025. One is a slight negative impact on demand growth overall. The other is a continuing effect of shifting volumes away from a few major centralized locations to more dispersed locations, in turn increasing the need for the main alliances to adjust their networks to reflect this dispersal as well as create opportunities for local niche carriers.

The final part of automation we will contemplate is the digitization. This is where processes related to the capture, transfer and process of information becomes automated.

This is a process which has been ongoing for a long time, with shipping lines having pursued the implementation of various types of eCommerce solutions to digitize principally the processes related to bookings, shipping instructions, freight documents and invoices. The state of affairs presently is quite mixed with some of these applications being good, and shipping lines seeing a high degree of usage, to shipping lines with no such applications at all.

If we look forward to 2025, this is an area wherein we are likely to see dramatic changes. As already mentioned previously, these changes will be driven by fundamental process changes, and not by IT. It is a shift which has already been described in the chapter pertaining to process management.

At the heart of the matter, the entire process related to information handling can be fully automated, as it is simply a matter of processing and distributing data between different systems and stakeholders. For successful shipping lines this will already be the case in 2025, although the degree of automation will be depending on the speed with which the cargo owners and shippers are able to transform. However, this is also partly a self-fulfilling prophecy. Shipping lines who become fully automated in this aspect will be more attractive to do business with for the cargo owners who are also becoming fully automated in their supply chain processes. Both parties will obtain efficiency savings from this, making both of them more competitive versus their respective competitors.

In essence, it is conceptually quite few processes which have to be automated, yet the current complexity in the details means that it will take time to accomplish.

Data provision to the shippers prior to booking must be automated. This means all provision of data related to the products being offered, the quality of the products and the price of the products.

Data capture from the shippers must be automated. This means all relevant data pertaining to a particular shipment, including booking data, shipping instructions, verified gross mass, relevant details on land side transportation when not handled by the shipping line etc.

Data provision to the shipper after booking must be automated. This includes booking confirmation, details on pick-up and drop-off of empty equipment. Provision of relevant freight documents, updates in case of service failures, issuance of invoices and collection of payments

Data exchange between the different operational processes within the shipping line must be automated. This includes data exchanges between equipment management, documentation, vessel operations, stowage, depots etc.

Data exchange with all external stakeholders must be automated. This includes terminals, port authorities, customs authorities, trucking form, railroad companies etc.

While this does appear daunting, it is very likely that the main shipping lines have managed to automate either all, or almost all, of these processes by 2025. And this is where the competitive situation becomes a main driver. It only requires one or two main shipping lines successfully accomplish this. In that case they would create a significant competitive advantage for themselves, and the other shipping lines will have the choice between automating themselves or finding themselves in a situation which is not viable in the long term.

Given that some lines are already further ahead than others, it means that the lines who are at the forefront will be in a position of competitive advantage as long as they can remain ahead on the development trajectory. Their advantage from automation will only disappear when all major shipping lines have reached a high level of automation.

Action Point: Automation

By 2025, a significant portion of the liner shipping fleet will be operated semi-autonomously. This means that the combination of sensors, real-time data streams and centralized computing power will be able to optimize the vessel operations and significantly reduce fuel consumption. This will necessitate a change in the role of captain.

The major container terminals will all be in various stages of semi-automation with the end-state for most being full automation. However in 2025 only a minority will have reached the stage of full automation.

The processes handling data flows will all become automated, however during the transition period from the current manual and semi-manual processes, shipping lines who are ahead on the automation trajectory will be at a competitive advantage until the other shipping lines reach the same level of maturity.

Finally, it should be clear to all stakeholders in the industry, that embarking upon automation without supporting it with improved process management is likely to reduce the value of automation significantly while increasing the risk of implementation failures.

Key questions:

What are your plans to equip your fleet with sensors and how do you plan to transmit the significant amounts of data?

How do you plan to process the data you obtain?

How do you plan to change the process on board the vessel in order for the computerized optimization models to have an impact on the actual vessel performance?

What is your plan for having all data flows being fully automated by 2025?

As a terminal, what is your long-term plan for full automation and what are your intermediary steps for semi-automation?

As a terminal, what issues do you foresee with local unions and how are you planning to address this?

As a terminal, how do you need shipping lines, truckers, railroad companies, port authorities, customs authorities to change in order to reap the full benefits of full or semi-automation?

Big Data

One cannot look at the developments in digitization without also looking at what has become known as Big Data. On the face of it, one would believe that Big Data is about analyzing large amounts of data, and using this to optimize the business. But, of course, reality is quite a bit more complex.

First of all, the value of Big Data is not primarily linked to the magnitude of the dataset, as the name otherwise appears to indicate. Clearly the sheer volume of data matters – if the dataset is very small, it is possible to analyze it using simple methods to start with. The importance about big data lies in the ability to integrate diverse datasets as well as unstructured datasets. For the shipping industry, a structured data set could for example be the data received from all the sensors on a semi-automated vessel. It could also be the collection of all bookings and shipping instructions received – although by other industry standards, the amount of data describing all bookings and shipping instructions is actually not all that big.

The unstructured datasets on the other hand is a new addition to the analytical tools. This could be qualitative feedback from sales representatives, entered into a Customer Relationship Database after each sales call. It could be automatic transcriptions of calls to customer service desks. Essentially, unstructured data are much more difficult to easily place into a database and use for the analysis. Additionally, some of the databases held by participants in the liner shipping industry, not just the shipping lines, have quite poor data quality. The poorer the data quality, the more the data needs to be analyzed as unstructured data.

Finally, Big Data becomes relevant when these large amounts of structured and unstructured data need to be analyzed in real-time in order to feed into decision making processes also taking place in real-time. This places a significant technical requirement on the construction of such systems.

At this point, a word of caution must be flagged. When one suddenly acquires the ability to build very large databases combined with the ability to look for patterns in these data, there is a significant temptation to do exactly that. However, this would be a mistake. Simply amassing a large amount of data and then search for patterns is a certain way to also find patterns. The problem is that the patterns may not be meaningful. It is the old adage of correlation without causation, and when a human mind spots a pattern, it is difficult to dispel this notion again, even if the correlation is meaningless. In simple examples it is easy to convince oneself that the correlation is meaningless.

A good way to develop a sense of proper caution with correlation without causation, is to look at the extensive sets of such examples readily available. One only need to take a look at sites such as tylervigen.com, showing how the per capita cheese consumption correlates with the number of people who die by becoming entangled in their bedsheets, or how the divorce rate in Maine correlates with the consumption of margarine.

This is not to disparage the value of Big Data. Big Data holds significant potential for the liner shipping industry to improve commercial performance. But it is to warn anyone embarking on Big Data that the way in which the analysis is developed is extremely important. With huge datasets, and analytical methods which are incomprehensible to most business managers, it is easy to be presented with highly convincing correlations, and not realize that it is correlation without causation.

The most risk-prone approach is to build a large database – or rather one would likely built a method for linking multiple disparate databases – and then start looking for patterns. This approach virtually guarantees that some of the patterns are without causality.

A more proper approach, which also requires a much more significant level of involvement in the design of the analysis, is to methodically apply the scientific method of making a hypothesis, and seeking to falsify this hypothesis through the use of the data. This will help to build solid models where there is a much stronger tie between correlation and causality. Once the models have passed the hurdle of acceptability, the Big Data "engine" can now be used to crunch the data in real-time, and thereby help improve commercial performance.

This also leads to another important aspect of Big Data. In order to get value from the output of the analysis, the recommendations from the model need to be implemented. This either requires fully automated systems which then respond to the output from the Big Data analysis, or a very strong process management within the company. Both of those cases come with risks though.

In the case of linking a Big Data analysis up to a fully automated system, the risk is increased for the system to suddenly stray from a planned behavior. This can happen when the input parameters into the Big Data analysis get outside the boundaries of the original design for the model. Ideally, a good model will be able to correctly analyse situations outside the initial training regime, but there is no sure way to know this. Therefore, whenever Big Data is linked to fully automated systems, it is imperative that an additional check is placed in the process to force a manual intervention, should the system suddenly deviate beyond certain given parameters.

In the case of linking Big Data into a manual process, the problem is almost the exact opposite of the fully automated system. In this case, a person is making decisions based on the recommendations from the Big Data system. As long as the system provides recommendations which are in line with the person's own expectations, these will be followed. However, when the recommendation deviate significantly between the model and the person, there is a strong tendency for the person to override the model, believing it to be wrong. This can happen also if the model operates within its original boundaries. The problem at hand might simply contain complex feedback mechanisms which the individual person is unaware of, but which the model captured accurately. In order to capture the value from Big Data in this case, it requires the implementation of very strong process controls, essentially forcing personnel to take action deemed correct by the model even when deemed incorrect by themselves. This is a very difficult management process and must be implemented upon solid analysis of the organization ramifications.

With these precautions in mind, where is it likely that Big Data will be in use in 2025?

The scope for use extends across a range of different applications, some of which we have already touched upon. Some are commercial in nature and some are operational.

On the operational side, the key use of Big Data relates to the optimization of vessel usage. First and foremost, it requires the vessels to be equipped with relevant sensors which provide a real-time stream of data on the performance. This will give a thorough overview of the fuel performance of the individual vessel, and can be used to reduce the operational costs for this individual vessel. But the Big Data scope goes beyond the individual vessel. Data will then be combined for all vessels within the context of the full network operated by the shipping line. Data pertaining to weather forecasts will be incorporated, as well as data from ports and terminals indicating the availability of berthing slots in cases where the vessels are delayed. Combining these data streams will provide the ability to analyze how to handle operational changes in a manner whereby the fuel costs are minimized in real time.

But the optimization can be taken even further. Data streams from inland operations, as well as customer behavior and preferences, can be taken into account. In the event of for example poor weather conditions shutting down a port, a shipping line might contemplate a choice between either waiting or skipping the port and going to the next port.

The Big Data system will calculate the most optimal choice taking into account not only the fuel consumption of the vessels, but also the costs of handling the exceptions which occur as a consequence of the choices – such as impact on feeders, added costs for inland transportation, commercial cost related to the customers perception of the choice etc.

Given the need to optimize fuel consumption from 2020, it is exceedingly likely that most major shipping lines will have real time systems in place before 2025 which allows the usage of Big Data to optimize fuel consumption even further. The main question for these shipping lines will be how to do it, and within which timescale they will be installing relevant sensors on the vessels.

The enhancement of the Big Data analytics to encompass the planning of optimal exception handling will also be in place by 2025, as that is the logical extension of the optimization of the individual vessel. However, given the complexities associated with this, not just analytically but in terms of the data quality needed, this is likely to be a second phase to be implemented fully when the first phase pertaining to the individual vessel optimization is finalized.

The second aspect of Big Data analytics is the use in combination with yield management. This requires shipping lines to have yield management processes fully firmed up and implemented, as otherwise any Big Data recommendations are likely not to be used in the existing pricing and capacity management processes.

Within yield management, the input data would comprise customer behavior – i.e. booking behavior, downfall behavior, customer behavior in relation to online pricing such as look-to-book ratios as well as analysis of competitor behavior in the context of own behavior. But it can be further leveraged by the inclusion of data streams from developments in the customers' own industries, such as anticipated changes in inventory levels as well as unstructured data feeds providing insights into aspects such as changes in manufacturing partners, strikes at factories or the creation of new distribution centers.

Additionally, the data can be combined with operational aspects such as the stowage planning tools, equipment availability at each depot, including the anticipated stock changes, and the cost and availability of truck, barge and rail services allowing a real-time modelling of the unit costs associated with the individual shipment.

All of this combined will result in the capability to provide much more accurate pricing which takes both accurate modelling of unit costs into account, as well as the anticipated competitive behavior. It is the path towards determining what the right freight rate is for each individual container given all the variables involved. As the markets proceed to commoditization on the main deep-sea trades, it is critical for the survival of a shipping line to be able to price correctly – and especially be able to spot every instance where it is possible to extract value from deviating from the commodity-driven underlying prices. Shipping lines which thrive in 2025 will be the ones who have such analytical power in place backed up by internal processes to ensure a solid implementation.

A third aspect of Big Data analytics revolves around empty equipment repositioning. Given both global and local trade imbalances, shipping lines will continue to move millions of empty containers around in order for them to be available where there are needed. Big Data analytics will provide the ability to optimize the flow, and thereby reduce the costs. For starters, it requires real-time data streams pertaining to the location of the individual container, obtained either through tracking devices on the containers or the ability to leverage internal operational systems together with AIS trackers on vessels, GPS trackers on trucks, gate-in and gate-out information from the ports and the equipment status in the container depots. This can be combined with both known and forecasted customer needs for full containers to allow not just the movement of empty containers to the right locations, but also to facilitate triangulated moves and match-back of empty containers, reducing the movements significantly. Such analytical systems will be standard by 2025, with simplistic trials of some of these aspects already taking place. Given the costs involved in empty repositioning, the question for the shipping lines in this context is not whether we will see the advent of Big Data analytics to improve equipment repositioning, the question is only how it will be done. In this context, the shipping lines have a fundamental choice to make.

They can choose to leverage the data internally and optimize their operations. Or they can choose to make the analytical data streams available to local 3rd party companies who might well be in a better position to use the data for optimization. A single shipping line is restricted in its optimization opportunities, whereas for example a 3rd party local trucking company would have the ability to triangulate the movements of his truck by combining the needs of multiple shipping lines. This leads to the next aspect. Given that local 3rd party transportation companies are able to tap into a larger value pool from the optimization better than any individual shipping line, these local companies would need analytical support systems as well to do this. The shipping lines could wait for this to happen, or they could actively participate in the development of such capabilities, as it would stand to benefit them as well.

The past decades' evolution of the alliances has shown, that shipping lines are indeed capable of collaboration when it results in leveraging a value pool neither line can harness on its own. Similarly, it is likely that by 2025 we will see the usage of Big Data systems on the land side which optimizes the usage of trucks, rail and barges to reduce both the cost of inland transportation in itself as well as minimizes the cost for empty repositioning. In this context, it might be advisable for the shipping lines to consider whether they want to be directly involved in the development of these systems or leave it to 3rd party providers. This is a choice which cannot be postponed until we get close to 2025. Instead this is a choice that needs to be made relatively soon as multiple different systems doing this is already under development.

Action Point: Big Data

By 2025, Big Data systems will have been developed and implemented focusing on improving vessel utilization for not just the individual vessel, but for the network in its entirety.

Yield management will be subjected to Big Data analytics, allowing the capability to identify when opportunities arise to price markedly different than the underlying commodity-driven pricing on the main trades.

Equipment repositioning and land-side container moves will be optimized through the usage Big Data systems spanning multiple shipping lines.

Key questions:

How do you plan to ensure that the correlation you find also represent actual causality?

How do you plan to get the people with the right skills to drive your Big Data strategy?

How do you plan to ensure that Big Data recommendations are not unduly overruled by decision makers who disagree with the recommendations?

How do you plan to ensure that decision makers, or automated systems, are capable of identifying when the Big Data recommendations are outside the scope of the model and cannot be trusted?

How do you plan to capture unstructured data from customer visits to enter into the yield management analytics?

How do you plan to address empty equipment and landside optimization – do you focus on internal optimization or do you participate in a multi-carrier approach possibly together with a 3rd party?

New Fuel Types

By 2020 the new low-Sulphur rules which were agreed in the International Maritime Organization will come into force. This effectively means that shipping lines will either have to switch to the more expensive low-Sulphur fuel, or they will have to install scrubbers, which come at a high initial capital expense. This will not only have the effect of further increasing the shipping lines' focus on reducing fuel consumption, but will also rekindle the focus on alternative fuel sources.

Until the rapid decline in bunker fuel prices at the end of 2014, the general shipping markets did see a growing interest in developing vessels fueled by LNG instead of traditional fuel oil. Even the liner shipping industry saw the orders of a few such vessels. Additionally, some of the new large vessels which were ordered were to a limited degree being designed to facilitate a later upgrade to LNG fuel. However, even at the high fuel oil prices at that time – around 700 USD per ton - LNG did not appear to be a cost effective option. The interest for LNG as a fuel was therefore more driven by future expectations for the 25-year lifespan of the vessels, than by more immediate economic considerations.

When one considers alternative fuel sources going forward, it is important to contemplate what would ultimately be the driving force, and how we are going to reach that stage. The usage of LNG fuel is cleaner from the perspective of for example the emissions of Sulphur and particulate matter than heavy fuel oil. It also emits less CO_2, but it clearly does emit CO_2. Hence the switch to LNG will solve some of the more immediate environmental priorities of the industry, but will not solve all of the long-term issues. In this case, however, long term reaches far beyond 2025.

In the very long term, the world appears to be on a path towards electrification. The reason for this is that electricity is independent of the energy source itself. As long as I have electricity available, the energy which developed it could have come from coal, oil, gas, solar, wind, nuclear or any other type of energy source. As an energy consumer, this means, that if I buy my energy in the form of electricity I can simply choose to get it from the cheapest source.

However, there are issues which are not fully resolved yet, but which are on a slow path towards being resolved. The first, and most critical issue relates to the storage of energy. If I have a manufacturing plant on land, I get my electricity from the power grid and I do not have a need to store energy. I leave that problem to the energy providers. But if I am in an industry with non-stationary assets, storage becomes a significant challenge. This applies particularly to road, ocean and air transport.

For the road transport, we have seen battery technology gradually evolve to the point where fully electric cars are now entirely feasible, although with a shorter range than comparable traditional cars. Nonetheless, the battery technology continues to evolve, both in terms of the energy storage capacity as well as in terms of how quickly it can be recharged. This means cars are already proceeding along a trajectory which will ultimately make them independent of energy source.

As this book is not about predicting exact technologies, but rather overall trends, it must be noted that a range of different energy storing technologies are competing. In addition to batteries, other types of fuel cells are being developed. Another example would be the use of hydrogen as a power source. The technological challenges in burning pure hydrogen safely are significant, and have not yet been overcome for practical commercial use. But in essence it is simply about using energy – from any source – to split water into Hydrogen and Oxygen. The Hydrogen can be stored, and when it is burned provide the energy we need, while emitting nothing but water from the process.

In the shipping industry, this development becomes of critical importance. The industry is following behind the auto industry, but the first vessels which incorporate combinations of traditional fuel and fuel cell technology are already in operation. Hence in terms of technology it is a matter of when the technology becomes sufficiently mature to be of practical use for the significant amounts of energy needed for the major liner shipping vessels.

This brings us back to the example in the very beginning of the book – the transition from sail to steam. Even if we see a significant breakthrough in for example fuel cell technology to the point where it becomes obvious to all that this is the technology of the future, the transition period will be measured in decades. As an absolute – and unrealistic – minimum, the transition time will be 20-25 years, which will correspond to a rapid shift where all newbuilds are equipped with the new technology and gradually the old technology disappears as the vessels are being scrapped.

This presents the shipping industry with a difficult dilemma in terms switching to LNG fuel. On one hand, LNG fuel has entered the realm of proven technology which can be installed on new vessels. It solves a range of the issues with emissions, and depending on the development in the oil price, may turn out to become a cheaper option due to the expected increases in gas production. From this perspective, it might indeed appear attractive to commence a transition process. In order for this to happen, we would also need to see major ports and terminals develop LNG fueling facilities for these new vessels. The most optimistic change-over process would then, as mentioned, be 20-25 years, with a complete fleet driven by LNG by around 2040.

The dilemma appears when we contemplate the timescale for the development of batteries or fuel cells or hydrogen powered ships or, in fact, any other technology which would allow for large-scale storage of energy. Once such a technology exists, it will change the game completely for the shipping industry. Not only will it eliminate all emissions from the vessels, but it will fundamentally alter the economic operating models as well. If large scale storage of energy becomes possible then, as mentioned, any energy consumer would simply be able to buy energy from the cheapest producer. If developments in renewable energy sources also continue on the trajectory we are currently at, the unit cost of energy will decline significantly in the long term. This is simply because the main costs associated with renewables are capital costs to build the facilities as well as maintenance costs. The energy itself is, by nature, free. In turn this leads to an ultimate situation where the variable cost to produce an added unit of energy approaches zero in theory. In practice this means extremely low energy costs. Not in the next 10 years, but in the long term.

For the shipping lines this means that LNG can never be more than a stepping stone. An intermediary step to a cleaner – but not renewable - fuel type, eventually to be replaced by a storage unit that makes the vessel independent of the energy type.

Then the long timeframes begin to matter. When will we see the switch to fuel cells?. If that is going to happen in 10-15 years, the gradual change-over to LNG as a fuel will in retrospect be seen as a costly mistake. We will have a fleet which is half-way replaced by LNG vessels, and ports and terminals will have made facilities to support this. The switch to the fuel cell vessels will at the same time be the switch to fuel which has almost zero marginal cost, and hence be extremely competitive compared to traditional vessels.

If, on the other hand, this technological shift does not happen until, for example, 2050 then the switch to LNG might indeed end up being a good business case, as the timeframe is sufficiently long to ensure a proper pay-off of vessels and port installations.

For the shipping lines about to order new vessels in the coming years, this means that they need to consider carefully what they believe the future will bring, and when it will happen. This has direct impact on whether to build traditionally fueled vessels, whether to switch to LNG or whether to hold out and use the 2ⁿᵈ hand market and charter ships until the fuel cell technology takes over.

For most shipping lines, the choice is not either-or. There will be immediate needs for traditional vessels, also in the coming years, but gradually the choice for the newer technologies will become more acute. And this is a matter to be contemplated not only by the shipping lines, but also by non-operating vessel owners as well as any financial entity who provides financing for a vessel with a 20-25 horizon.

Action Point: New Fuel Types

By 2025, the vast majority of the fleet in operation will be using traditional fuel types, although appropriate changes being made to abide by the low-Sulphur rules.

However, it is plausible that we have also seen the beginning of a shift to LNG powered vessels, and if that is the case it will likely have been spearheaded by smaller feeder vessels where the fuel consumption per container makes the investment case even more attractive than for the ultra-large vessels. Additionally, when we get beyond 2020, a sizeable part of the global fleet of feeder vessels reaches an age of 25 years and are due for replacement.

The dilemma of whether LNG fuel will be overtaken by fuel cells before a fleet-wide switch to LNG will at this point likely have been settled. Either it is clear that fuel cell (or similar battery or other technology) becomes commercially viable for the vessels inside a horizon of 5-10 years – which requires several actual vessels have been in operation for a while. Or the technology remains at a prototype stage which would push an actual transition out 10-15 years at least, paving the way for a larger transition to LNG.

Key questions:

How to you contemplate the change in fuel technology when you evaluate the life-time value of a new build vessel?

If you are contemplating a switch to LNG powered vessels, what is your exist strategy should other technologies leapfrog you?

If you are not switching to LNG, how do you plan to abide by the increasingly strict environmental rules and regulations towards 2025?

Are you planning to become actively engaged in the testing of new fuel technologies?

Transforming Ports and Terminals

Container ports and terminals will see significant changes in the period to 2025, partly driven by the changes in the shipping lines, partly by the demographic developments and partly by their own internal competition.

We have at this point touched on these topics individually, with notes reflecting on the ports and terminals. In this chapter, the overall development patterns are combined.

The main development we are likely to see, is a significant fight for market share over the coming years driven by all of the aforementioned changes. By 2025, this battle will have been largely settled with the outcome being a range of larger local ports, further expansion of some major transshipment hubs, and a significant decline in volumes for other transshipment hubs. Hence the coming years will be critical for the future of many ports and terminals.

The drive towards automation, which goes through various stages of semi-automation, is a path an increasing number of terminals is already going down. Given the efficiencies associated with this, it will continue to happen. The consequence of the automation is a de-facto increase in terminal capacity. Well-planned automation results in faster vessel handling, faster turn-times for pick-up and drop-off on the land side and increased capacity at the terminal's area for container storage. As the overall market for container transportation will exhibit relatively modest growth, the automation alone will absorb a sizeable part of the organic growth.

The second aspect is the effect of the major container shipping alliances. These alliances result in the ability to improve the network design by having more direct port-pairs covered, in turn reducing the incidence of transshipments. This does not by any stretch of the imagination mean that transshipment is going to disappear – the backbone networks driven by mega-vessels will clearly continue to have a need for transshipments, but it does mean that volumes specifically for transshipment are likely to see a negative development.

The larger alliances will result in larger transshipment volumes at key hubs, and if a hub operation is to be as efficient as possible, it ideally requires all vessel operations to take place in the same terminal. Some ports have multiple different terminals, and this lead to a challenge whereby very few terminals are capable of handling the full volumes from an alliance.

An added point to this is analysis performed by the company LinerGrid, which has detailed modelling capabilities for the design of global container shipping networks, shows that there are clear benefits associated with a limited number of major transshipment hubs as opposed to a wider range of hubs – provided that such terminals can handle the operational volumes.

These considerations from a network design perspective leads to the conclusion that the major terminals are facing a high-stakes game in the next few years. Locking in the volumes from a major alliance will also ensure large volumes, especially as operates might see the number of key hubs reduce. On the other hand, failure to land the major part of an alliance can well result in a negative spiral where the terminal will see the loss of feeder services – as there is now less cargo to transship. This in turn makes the hub less attractive to the alliance as they now are less well connected to the outports, and the downwards spiral has begun. This is a downwards spiral which is a genuine risk for a large range of major existing hubs in the period towards 2025.

Another challenge which the ports are already facing, but which will accelerate in the coming years, is the shipping lines' phase-in of ever larger vessels. As previously shown this is not only about the 18-21.000 TEU vessels, it is about all vessel sizes due to the cascading of vessels from one trade to another. Ports and terminals are therefore being met with requirements from the shipping lines to be able to handle larger vessels. This typically requires investments in bigger cranes, longer quays and deeper draft. This is problematic in an environment where cargo volumes only grow slowly.

One hand the port will be responding to a genuine customer need – i.e. the need to handle bigger vessels. On the other hand the port is not necessarily going to see much more cargo move through the port as a consequence of the upgrade. Additionally, the shipping lines will be seeking a cost reduction on account of the efficiency gains associated with handling fewer, but larger vessels.

The combination of these events leads towards a situation of significant overcapacity, especially across transshipment ports. As terminals are fixed assets which cannot be moved anywhere else – unlike the vessels – their options will be quite limited. As the downside risk for a terminal is a significant – or complete – loss of cargo volume, the incentive to reduce prices to maintain cargo volume is high. Furthermore, as these are assets with lifetimes measured in decades, the argument to the owners will be that this might be loss-making right now, but in the long term the investment will still be good.

Finally, as secondary ports in emerging markets are in the process of upgrading their port facilities to handle vessels in the range of 8-12.000 TEU, this increases the opportunities the shipping lines to broaden their networks to have more direct port coverage. For the transshipment hubs, this development will add a negative pressure on their volumes.

For such secondary ports, it might seem like a significant upside, however this is not necessarily the case. First of all, the cargo is already being handled in these ports – albeit by feeder vessels instead of main line vessels. The upside only appears if the improved port infrastructure succeeds in driving trade growth to be higher than average. This in turn means that these ports have to be in locations which are aligned with the demographic shifts that we will be witnessing over the coming decade.

The final aspect to consider in this context is the potential impact of China's One Belt, One Road (OBOR) strategy. Essentially it is a long-term strategy likely to unfold on a timescale beyond 2025 and aim at creating a supply chain infrastructure tying East Asia, Central Asia, Africa and the eastern parts of Europe and the Mediterranean much closer together. The published plans for OBOR remains relatively high level, and the initiatives which has gotten the most attention thus far is more related to overland supply chains and less to shipping. However, the plans make it clear the port infrastructure is a component of OBOR as well. This in turn means that ports and terminals in this, large, area are exposed to an opportunity and a threat at the same time. For some ports located in areas designated of strategic importance for OBOR, this can result in improved access to investment funds in order to create more port and terminal capacity. For other ports not on the OBOR grid, this could mean the exposure to intensified competition from ports who did indeed manage to get such investment funds. In either case, this development – if pursued at a rapid pace – would only add to the building pressure of overcapacity in the terminal sector.

Action Point: Ports and Terminals

By 2025, we will be at the end stage of a competitive development which will have seen a global reduction in the transhipment incidence, and the consolidation of transhipment volumes into fewer key hub. This will result in some ports having grown significantly beyond their current sizes, and other having seen significant declines.

All main terminals, especially transhipment terminals will be significantly down the path of semi-automation, although not necessarily fully automated. This is covered more in the automation chapter.

Key questions:

For transhipment terminals, what is your level of competitiveness versus other transhipment terminals – and how do you plan to attract more volume?

For import/export terminals, how do you plan to balance the need to cater for larger vessels against a limited growth in actual cargo volumes?

For ports and terminals in the OCOR region, how do you plan to either become an active part of the overall OBOR initiative in the long term or how do you plan to compete with ports that are?

For all ports and terminals, how do you plan to address the fact that alliances get larger and volumes therefore more concentrated on fewer entities?

Changing the IT Landscape

As mentioned earlier, this book is not focused on specific technological solutions and will therefore not address specific IT systems or solutions either.

However, the underlying dynamics of the IT landscape in the industry will change. Or, what might be a more accurate depiction, the shipping lines which manage to fundamentally change their IT landscapes will still have the opportunity to be here in 2025.

The IT landscape encompasses much more than just hardware and software. More importantly it encompasses the ability to translate business processes into IT requirements, it is the ability to implement solutions into the actual organization, it is the ability to become agile and change at a pace matching changes in the surroundings, it is about being able to test new concepts quickly and it is the ability to recognize when individual solutions should be discarded in favor of global standards and solutions.

The first step to successfully transform the IT landscape is to ensure a strong culture of process management within the company. This is an aspect which has already been covered in the prior chapter about process management and will thus not be covered in detail here. Essentially a lack of process management makes it very difficult not only to develop well-functioning systems, but also to implement the usage of systems into the organization if they are based on the requirement that traditional ways of handling the business must change.

This is the point where disruptors from outside established companies typically make their mark. Disruptors often appear to be successful because they have a new IT system, program or application. However, what happens is typically that they have found an entirely different way to handle the process of servicing the customer. A process which is significantly more efficient, and which is flawlessly implemented into an organization unencumbered by how notions of how business is supposed to be done.

Looking at how the shipping lines have implemented eCommerce over the past 15 years in the industry, the pattern is typically seen to be one of perpetuating existing ways of doing business. Individual sub-components of the business processes are being transformed into IT systems, in themselves creating savings, but at the same time not fundamentally improving the ways of doing business.

The industry has now begun to embrace the notion of digitization, but for many shipping companies this appears to be driven primarily out of a need not to be left behind by a combination of the few shipping lines who are moving quickly in this arena as well as by potential external 3rd party disruptors. The shipping lines have correctly ascertained, that failure to embark on a path to digitization will drastically reduce their likelihood of being a successful company 2025, but the greatest risk at this stage is for them to see digitization primarily as the need to build IT systems.

This is a risk because the development of IT systems is a more visible manifestation of action than the more intangible aspect of process management. But lines would do well in remembering that IT systems are only the practical manifestation of the underlying process management, and if these are not well thought out, then neither will the IT systems.

A second aspect related to the IT systems becomes one of agility. Agility both within the development of the IT systems as well as agility in the implementation of the systems.

As the industry undergoes the digitization transformation over the coming years, nobody can today predict exactly what the solutions will look like. Traditionally the shipping lines have created very large systems to support their business, with these systems becoming back bones of the business in some cases literally for decades. In a situation where it is clear that change must happen, but the exact nature of that change is more uncertain, it is imperative that the new IT landscape is developed in such a way that changes can be made quite quickly, which in turn translates into specific requirements for the design of the underlying IT architecture. In this respect, the risk is almost the same as for process management. Just as for process management, IT architecture is essentially an invisible part of the IT landscape, and for many business focused leaders it is much easier to see the effects of digitization on a customer-facing application than on a back-end architecture design. But it is the architecture which provides the platform for agility.

Secondly, given the significant uncertainties surrounding the future manifestation of digitization, shipping lines should abstain from trying to follow the path of first designing the perfect solution, then building the solution and finally implementing the solution. Instead they need to embrace a method whereby new applications are developed into prototypes very quickly, and then those prototypes are implemented as pilot tests in small contained parts of the market. This allows for quick feedback from the market itself as to whether the solution works or not, as well as how to alter the approach to improve it. Likewise, if a solution is seen not to work, the shipping line should also be quick to terminate the pilot again. Terminating a pilot should not be seen as failure – not launching multiple pilots should instead be seen as a failure.

We should therefore expect a development in the coming years where an array of different solutions are being launched into the liner shipping market. Many of these solutions will be partly overlapping in their scope. Some will appear radically different from the current way of doing business. Over time many of these will disappear again, and when we reach 2025, we will have seen the most successful ones emerge to shape the practical implementation of digitization.

Shipping lines should regard it as a strategic priority to be able to develop and launch such pilot projects, and at the same time have the project management controls in place to quickly determine which projects to continue to develop, and which projects to shut down again.

Secondly, they also need to have a communication strategy in connection with these pilots. Communication towards the market in general is of course necessary, and in an industry not used to agile pilot tests of IT systems, it is very likely that some of these pilots will be over-interpreted by market as being more than just pilots. Managing the market expectation is therefore necessary to avoid an undue backlash when pilots are closed down due to non-performance.

A critical component is equipping the front-end sales and customer service staff with the proper understanding of how to communicate. Staff which is directly involved in the running of the pilot will of course know the scope and ramifications, but all other staff members will also be asked about this, and it can quickly undermine a pilot if not managed properly. As an example, consider a shipping line which is running a pilot focused on low-cost pricing in exchange for a stand-by slot on the vessel. I.e. the customer gets a good price, the shipping line only guarantees that the container will be loaded with 14 days of gate-in depending on which vessel has open capacity. In this case, sales staff which is not involved the pilot might be contacted by customers seeking to use the online price as negotiation leverage to reduce the price on the standard products. This is where the staff need to be properly briefing on how to handle such situations, otherwise this could undermine not just the individual pilot, but the company's ability to carry out pilots in general.

Action Point: IT Landscape

By 2025 we will have seen a new IT landscape emerge which is characterized by being agile and process driven.

For the shipping lines, the critical period in relation to this change is in the coming years, and this is where they need to transform their approach. Simply put, shipping lines which approach this transformation from the perspective that this is all about buying a new customer-facing IT system, or a fantastically looking application, but without fundamentally addressing the process issue and the IT architecture are exceedingly likely to fail in the long term transformation.

Key questions:

How do you plan to improve your agility in terms of building, deploying and piloting new systems and applications?

How do you define agility within your company?

How do you plan to develop the capability to run multiple pilot tests simultaneously without interfering with the mainstream business?

How do you plan to make a seamless interaction between design the business process, designing the IT systems and implementing the solution and process within the organization?

Changes for Cargo Owners

The changes described for the transformation in the industry to 2025 will have significant ramifications for the cargo owners as well. At the end of the day, the cargo owners are the true customers given that they are the ones who have a need for their cargo to be transported. Any attempt at transformation which leads to a significant degradation of value for the cargo owners will therefore be met with failure.

But, as we have seen, the path to a successful transformation involves the use of multiple pilot tests as shipping lines test various ideas. Some ideas will turn out to have significant theoretical value, but may fall flat in practical use. Other ideas might involve a very large change in business process, also for the cargo owner, and might appear not to be worthwhile – but at the end of the day might turn out to be just the right solution.

Furthermore, with millions of cargo owners ranging from very small to very large, all with highly diverse needs, it is clear that there will not be just one standard solution which fits everyone. Multiple solution will be part of the landscape.

Some cargo owners will want to have a seamless integration between their own backend ERP systems and the shipping lines. Others will want the ability to quickly get an overview of the market, get the cargo booked and shipped out the door. Some will want the ability to "play the market" as they might find themselves able to forecast market developments better than others, and therefore focus entirely on the spot market. Some cargo owners need stability and will be looking for the ability to have iron-clad enforceable contracts in place. The examples are almost endless.

During this transformation process, cargo owners therefore need to become actively involved as well. As shipping lines are launching pilots of various concepts, the cargo owners need to assess whether the pilot might provide a value proposition which would be of interest to them. If that is the case, they should actively seek to become part of the pilot, testing the new concept. This is the only way for them to ensure that the new products and processes which are being developed will ultimately fit their own purposes.

For a cargo owner, it is easy to decide not to engage at the pilot stage. After all, the product is not final yet, and might right from the start show some obvious flaws. The cargo owner could therefore easily decide to sit on the sidelines and await a more well-polished final solution before engaging.

However, failure to engage in the pilots can result in one of two outcomes. In one case, the shipping lines determine that the concept which the pilot is supposed to test is not interesting for the customers, and then it is quickly shut down. The cargo owner who saw the solution as promising, but not final, will have lost the opportunity to get a product he is genuinely interested in. In the other case, other cargo owners engage in the pilot, which helps shape the final product. However, these cargo owners might have different needs from the ones who chose to sit on the sidelines. Again, this results in a negative impact on the cargo owners who chose not to be involved.

Once the learning points from the pilots begin to solidify, we will see the emergence of a limited range of standardized solutions. Clearly there will be niche applications emerging as well, but for the majority of cargo owners, the emergence of the new standard ways of doing business will happen before 2025. Once these standards solidify, the cargo owners' processes for handling the supply chain will also change in order get the most value from the new processes. Supply chain managers need to be aware of this and actively work within their own organizations to get this implemented.

The final approach a cargo owner can take is to use this opportunity to actively approach shipping lines and suggest ideas for new business processes and applications, and thus become active drivers of process innovation. Or, depending on the nature of the idea, approach 3rd party companies who can take it upon themselves to develop such new business ideas, and through them engage the shipping lines.

Action Point: Cargo Owners

The digitized landscape in 2025 will not designed overnight. In the coming years we will see a range of different solutions emerge, some competing, some highly diverse. Cargo owners need to actively participate in pilots in order to ensure that the future landscape becomes designed based on actual market needs and behaviours, and not purely on solutions which may appear attractive in theory.

Whilst a strategy of waiting on the side lines until the new landscape emerges might appear to be the sound low-risk approach, in reality if carries significant risks for the cargo owners. In this case, the solutions which are standard in 2025 will have been dominated by the needs of a select group of first-movers amongst the cargo-owners, whereas the risk-averse cargo owner will have had much less influence. However, given the diversity amongst cargo owners, it is unlikely that the needs of the first-movers exactly match the needs of more risk-averse companies. Thus, in reality, the prudent low-risk strategy in relation to the transformation towards 2025 is to actively engage with the shipping lines in the pilots.

Key questions:

How do you identify which pilot(s) to engage in?

How much of your cargo do you wish to have involved in the pilot(s)?

How would we ideally want to see the market in 2025 – and are the currently development supporting this? If not, how do we plan to engage the shipping lines or 3rd parties to make this happen?

Changes for Forwarders and NVOCCs

Forwarders and NVOCCs, as well as other business models in various forms which bridge the gap between the cargo owners and the shipping lines, stand to be significantly impacted by the digitization process towards 2025. Whether positively or negatively depends partly on their current business model and partly on the transformation process they plan to undertake.

At the simple end of the scale we have those NVOCCs which merely sell simple transactional transportation products. This is the kind of product which will see the largest pressure from the digitization process as not only the port-port products become transparent and easy to book online, but as the tie-in of trucking service at origin and destination becomes part of that online transactional product as well. The ability to extract a margin from this business will become severely eroded, as customers will be able to handle the simple transportation themselves.

Secondly, part of the business model for these NVOCCs have been to buy significant volumes from the shipping lines at a low price due to the volume commitment, and sell it in smaller portions at a marked-up price. But as shipping lines manage to combine scientific yield management principles with the online commercial platforms, the shipping lines will be able to ascertain the correct price point for the small customers themselves, as well as have the ability to sell directly to them. Therefore, this type of business model will be under severe pressure towards 2025.

As we increase the complexity of the product offered by freight forwarders to include elements such as supply chain management, warehousing services, packing and stuffing services etc., the impact of the digitization process changes in nature. Not only are some of these supply chain services exceedingly difficult to automate, they also tend to be tailor-made to suit specific needs for specific customers. In this case the advent of digitization is an opportunity for the freight forwarders.

The improved transparency of the cargo movements allows them to deliver supply chain visibility products with a much higher degree of timeliness and accuracy than what is currently possible. In turn this also allows them to design, and manage, a supply chain with a higher degree of efficiency than what is currently possible.

The improved transparency in pricing might at first glance appear to undermine the forwarders' ability to extract a margin. As such the starting point should be, that the pricing of supply chain products must be based on the value created through supply chain management, and not through a simple mark-up on the transactional price.

Another aspect of the transformation which furthers the business model of the freight forwarders, is the shipping lines' drive towards commoditization, which in turn shifts the competition increasingly towards exception management. This is a topic we have already considered in one of the previous chapters. An individual carrier will compete on its ability to handle exceptions as they occur, however will to some degree be limited by the fact that it is "only" one carrier. A freight forwarder will have more options with which to deal with exceptions, being able to leverage products across a range of shipping lines. This is to some degree what forwarders already do, but the advent of improved supply chain visibility tools in real time, as well as the advent of tools to help forecast service failures will provide freight forwarders with added opportunities to leverage such services.

Given that the ability to handle exceptions at times need detailed local knowledge, this means that small local freight forwarders might experience the digitization as a significant opportunity as well – provided that their business models focus on providing such value-added services.

In the short term, the growth in online platforms designed to sell transactional transportation services might be a boost to small local forwarders who will see it as a means to expand their marketing reach and be able to service customers on a cost-efficient manner. These small local companies are very agile and will be able to leverage these tools more quickly than the major shipping lines. However, as the shipping lines slowly get their yield management processes in place, these small forwarders will find this part of the business being eroded. The benefit to this segment will therefore largely be in the short to medium term, but will have been severely eroded by 2025.

Finally, the freight forwarders need to engage with the shipping lines in terms of piloting new solutions – in this respect the pros and cons for forwarders are almost identical to those outlined for the cargo owners, but of course they would need to see different aspects of the supply chain improved.

Action Point: Freight Forwarders and NVOCCs

The transparent and digitized landscape in 2025 will have severely eroded any business models for intermediaries based on a simple mark-up freight, irrespective of whether this mark-up today was based on market intransparency or whether it was based on a wholesale model of buying large volume commitment at a unit cost discount.

On the other hand, the improved visibility pertaining to both cargo movements as well as service failures will increase the freight forwarders ability to offer services based on a combination of tailor-made logistics solutions which are hard to automate and the ability to perform exception management across a range of shipping lines.

In the short to medium term intermediaries might see a surge in business models where they leverage online transportation solutions for simple transactional cargo. This is because they may be able to act faster, and in a more agile way, than the shipping lines. However, this is likely to be a temporary phase, and these models will be under severe pressure when the shipping lines become able to handle yield management processes in an efficient manner.

Key questions:

How do I plan to change my business model to not rely on a freight mark-up?

How do I plan to leverage my ability to handle exceptions in an environment of full transparency of freight movements as well as of service failures?

If I plan to leverage the online sales of transportation services in the short term by being more agile than the shipping lines, what is then my exit strategy to ensure the early gains are not offset by late-stage losses?

It is all about the people and the culture

For a shipping line to undergo the transformation which has been described, this requires a commitment to change impacting not only the individuals in the company, but also the much more intangible – and crucial – a change in the companies' cultures.

Let us look at the individuals first. As already described previously, the digitization is going to result in a significant reduction in staffing levels in 2025 compared to the current situation. This in itself will be a cause for resistance in any organization trying to embrace the changes. It has to be expected, that changes in business processes which will lead to the elimination of jobs, will result in people internally in the company providing arguments as to why proposed changes are unlikely to work, and hence should not be implemented. Furthermore, in some countries the implementation of these changes is likely to be challenged by unions with the power to slow down the process.

To handle this development, it is imperative that the companies plan the transformation well in terms of how to handle the human aspect, and making sure that their organizations understand not only how the changes are going to happen, by why they need to happen. At the end of the day, failure to make a transformation will drastically reduce the likelihood that the company will exist in 2025.

The transformation also means that new types of people need to be brought into the organizations. These will be people will skillsets matching more specialized functions in the digitized transportation companies. They will tend to have higher educations focused on topics such as for example online design and interactions, communication, advanced analytics, process management and the development of IT requirements.

The shipping lines need to contemplate how they will convey an understanding of the fundamental business to these new people. The starting point is that these new employees bring a set of skills which the company itself does not have – and realistically many inside the company will at the outset not necessarily know how to fully utilize the skills these people bring into the organization. But the starting point is also that these new people do not have an understanding of the basics of the industry they have entered.

The shipping line must therefore ensure that these people are provided with a thorough understanding of how the industry works. Not only do they need to know how the industry works, they also need to know the quirks and idiosyncrasies inherent in the industry. Only by providing them with this knowledge will they be able to leverage their own skills for the improvement of the overall business model. A failure to understand how the industry works presently ultimately results in a failure to understand whether new ideas are even feasible – or what it takes to make them feasible.

Once these new people have acquired the necessary background knowledge of the industry, they need to be actively involved in the pilots of the new solutions. This is where the new ideas are tested and modified, and this is where the new people will work integrated with the more traditional shipping people in creating the baseline for automation and digitization.

When we then move from the individual person to the collective of people which makes up an entire company, this is where company culture becomes important.

In the shipping lines' quest to transform themselves over the next decade, they need to take a close look at their own company culture and identify where the transformation process might require a change. This is a process which can be much more difficult and protracted than one might initially appreciate. In the book "Culture Shock in Maersk Line" written by the same author as this book, it is described how Maersk

Line went through a significant transformation process in order to be able to embrace key elements of process management. This journey was not smooth – and, in reality, it took several years even to get the journey started.

The challenge is that the processes, and business models, needed to accomplish the transformation which has been outlined in this book for 2025 requires changes that goes to the heart of many shipping lines' culture. As a very basic example, it changes the concept of loyalty. Many shipping companies have a history of being run be a very small group of people, despite having many employees. In these companies, loyalty is often held in high regard, and is an important trait. The transformation these companies are facing will not eliminate loyalty – but will change the object of the loyalty. In a process driven company, the processes which has been developed and implemented has to be followed – or it has to be specifically make clear which exceptions to handle outside the main stream processes. This means the especially middle-managers will have to be loyal to the process, as otherwise they will undermine the whole drive towards digitization and automation. This can often be misinterpreted as a loss of loyalty to the customers and a loss of loyalty to senior managers. It requires the middle manager at times to tell his superior that a certain decision should be reconsidered as it undermines the processes. It requires a discussion with a customer who has been a loyal customer for years, but who now find that his special exception can no longer be accommodated.

And here we are at one of the keys to making the successful transformation – involving the staff at all levels during this process, as otherwise the transformation will be undermined. Let us stay with the example of the loyal customer. The customer has historically found that the exception made for him provided him with value. Suddenly he is being told by the customer service manager that this is no longer the case because the people in headquarters have designed a process that makes it impossible. This is a sure-fire way to undermine one's own business and derail the transformation process.

Instead, as clearly outlined in the chapter about exceptions, a shift to process management necessitates the identification of how to define and deal with exceptions. This has to be developed at the same time as the processes – not as an afterthought when the customer service representative meets the angry customer. This leads to the next step that the staff, all the way to the front-end, has to be involved in the entire process, and not simply be presented with a blue print from headquarters. In that case, they will need to present all the arguments for why certain types of exceptions should be made, and this forms the baseline for which exceptions will be handled outside the main process. It also means that when they are being told that their specific client cannot get his exception, there is a rational explanation outlining exactly why the company will no longer accommodate this request – it might be the very simple reason that it is too costly to provide that specific exception, and the vessels could be filled with other cargo not requiring that specific exception. Other carriers might have defined exceptions differently, leading back to the previously mentioned point that by 2025, the ability to handle exceptions becomes a competitive differentiator.

This was only a single small example. The journey of cultural transformation experienced by Maersk Line provides a baseline view of how such a journey can be undertaken in a liner shipping company – and also how the transformation to the new times in the industry is often a difficult one requiring decisions which are not always well liked by neither customers nor employees.

Action Point: People and culture

In 2025 shipping lines will have organizations which are more top-heavy, simply because a large amount of positions which are today back-office functions will have become automated. At the same time, they will consist of a range of people with skills that are today almost absent in the shipping companies. In order to get to that point, it is important to have a plan for the onboarding of the new people -

especially for those who are envisioned to gradually grow into senior positions. At the same time it is necessary to contemplate how the scale-down of staff will take place in times of automation without demoralizing staff – simply because the automation will not happen overnight, but be a long and gradual process.

Key questions:

Given the transformation you are planning to undertake, what will your organization look like in 2025?

Which new key positions in that organization do I need to groom through my internal pipeline, and when to I need to start doing that?

How do I on-board people with expertise in digitization, automation, process management etc. but who has no shipping knowledge?

How to I maintain staff morale for a protracted period as automation slowly reduces job opportunities in the company?

What is the core components of my company culture? Which of these components will hinder the transformation towards 2025? And how will I bridge this gap in the next decade?

Is There Another Way?

By know it should be clear that change is indeed coming, as well as what that change entails for the liner shipping industry in terms of the underlying trends.

For some companies, the reaction to this might be one of denial. This is all in the future, and the future might develop in a different way than envisioned. Forecasts are often not accurate. This is indeed the case, and it is also why this book is not obsessed with numbers and graphs, because it is de-facto impossible to predict whether the demand will grow by 2% or 4% or indeed decline by 4%. That does not change the fact that such quantitative forecasts must be made for tactical planning purposes, but irrespective of the actual number, the underlying trends we have considered for the changes to 2025 are largely the same irrespective of how the actual numbers develop.

The numbers are about optimizing the business in the short to medium term, and for this, different companies will need to place emphasis on different types of numbers. They will need forecasts for their specific focus points, not general all-sweeping numbers like the global demand growth rate.

However, for the long-term strategic changes, these will take place in the presence of some larger macro trends, such as digitization and automation, and the main uncertainty about these changes is not whether they will happen, but only within which timeframe they will happen, and what the precise practical manifestation of them will be.

Another aspect that might be raised is the simple question: Is there another way?

For some shipping lines, and cargo owners, the notion of a process-driven automated future might not only appear daunting, but downright negative. This might go against everything a company stands for in terms of specialized services and close relationship with individual clients. In this case, it is worth keeping in mind that, as already mentioned previously, niche markets will continue to exist. However, if a shipping line wants to remain, or become, a niche carrier they still need to analyze the structural changes and identify whether their intended niche will be a defensible niche or not in a future where many of their competitors will have transformed.

Interestingly, the question of "Is there another way" is likely the one being asked across a range of smaller entrepreneurial companies with a specific aim to disrupt the liner shipping industry. They look at an industry with cumbersome processes as well as an enormous amount of layers and middle men, and they see significant opportunities for devising "another way". However, this other way will fall into the overall categories already discussed, and hence we are back to the starting point – if the shipping lines want to remain relevant as major forces in the global shipping industry they need to embark on a journey of transformation, or someone else will do it to them.

What are the next steps?

The next steps which every stakeholder in the industry need to contemplate are in principle easy, but in practice quite complicated.

They need to create a clear understanding of where they want to be in 2025 – not as much in terms of precise cargo volumes and fleet sizes, but more in terms of what their fundamental business model will be and what it will require for the business model to be profitable.

Once that fixpoint is created, the next step involves analyzing the current status of the company when seen specifically in relation to the desired position in 2025. Again, this is less about numbers and more about business models, processes and culture. With this baseline the analysis – which will be different for every different company – needs to focus on what it takes to change the current status into the future desired status. Many of the questions which need to be asked are the ones outlined at the end of each chapter in this book.

Only when this plan is made should the next level of detail be involved – that is the level of details which includes quantitative forecasts of demand patterns, network changes, customer preferences, new vessel designs, whether to grow organically or by acquisition etc. This is the step of the strategy where the number have to add up so to speak – but the preliminary work on the transformation of the business models is the baseline upon which this strategy has to rest.